THE
MANAGEMENT
BIBLE

THE
MANAGEMENT
BIBLE

BOB NELSON
PETER ECONOMY

WILEY

John Wiley & Sons, Inc.

Published by John Wiley & Sons, Inc., Hoboken, New Jersey.
Published simultaneously in Canada.

For general information on our other products and services please contact our Customer Care Department within the United States at (800) 762-2974, outside the United States at (317) 572-3993 or fax (317) 572-4002.

Wiley also publishes its books in a variety of electronic formats. Some content that appears in print may not be available in electronic books. For more information about Wiley products, visit our web site at www.wiley.com.

Library of Congress Cataloging-in-Publication Data:

Nelson, Bob, 1956–
    The management bible / Bob Nelson and Peter Economy.
        p.   cm.
    ISBN 0-471-70545-4 (pbk.)
    1. Management—Handbooks, manuals, etc.   II. Title.
    HD38.15.N45   2005
    658.4—dc22

                                                    2004022893

Printed in the United States of America.

10   9   8   7   6   5   4   3   2   1

Contents

✿ **PART V:** **Management Challenges**

Introduction

People talk a lot about how the world of business has changed; how markets today are not just regional or national, but global; how fast-evolving telecommunications technology has dramatically cranked up the speed of doing business; and how employees are seeking more meaningful work along with a voice in the decisions that affect them. It's true, the world of business has changed. More than ever before, this means that managers must also change to meet these new challenges.

> The old ways of managing employees are broken. Here's how to fix them (and become a better manager in the process).

Whether you're new to management or a seasoned pro, you'll find every topic you need to be an exceptional manager addressed here—from hiring the best employees to motivating, coaching, and mentoring them; from setting goals to executing plans and holding employees accountable; from working with teams to disciplining employees. In short, this is one of the most comprehensive, yet up-to-date and clearly explained guides available today on the topic of management.

In this book, we take the topic of management to a new level by giving you doses of reality from business in several features that run through the book:

- *The Real World* cuts to the chase in explaining how things *really* work on each of the topics discussed. You'll have the opportunity to short-circuit your learning process and benefit from our many years of experience, both as managers and as writers on the topics of management and leadership.

- *The Big Picture* provides a cutting perspective from some of the top business leaders as to what they view is most important to achieving success as a manager in the fast-changing global business environment. Presented in a question-and-answer interview format, these leaders are frank about challenges they've dealt with and lessons they've learned in their management careers.
- *Ask Bob and Peter* features real questions we've received from managers across the country and abroad about a wide variety of issues. Chances are you'll find the answers to some of your own challenges in these responses.

We hope you enjoy this book and find it useful in helping you to be a better manager. For more information, please visit our web sites at (for Bob) www.nelson-motivation.com and (for Peter) www.petereconomy .com. We would also welcome any feedback or questions you have, and you can contact Bob directly via e-mail at bobrewards@aol.com.

We'd love to hear from you, and we wish you all the best in your management journey.

Bob Nelson
San Diego, California

Peter Economy
La Jolla, California

The Art and Science of Management

CHAPTER 1

What Managers Do

IT'S A NEW WORLD OUT THERE . . .

Functions and . . .

How they allow managers to get things done through others.

The classic functions of management.

Energizing employees and unleashing their potential.

Empowerment rules!

Your employees need your support.

Communication makes the world go 'round.

WHAT MANAGERS ARE SUPPOSED TO DO

One of the first questions new managers ask—even if only themselves—is: What am I supposed to do now?

Traditionally, when new managers *are* provided with an answer to this question (often they aren't; they are simply hired or promoted to manager with no training or direction whatsoever), the answer has been the four *classic functions* of management that you may have learned in school—planning, organizing, leading, and controlling.

- *Planning:* Running an organization is kind of like steering a ship on the ocean; to get where you want to go, you've got to have a plan— a map—that tells you where you're headed. It's the job of managers to develop the plans that determine the goals an organization will pursue, the products and services it will provide, how it will manufacture and deliver them, to whom, and at what price. These plans include creating an organizational vision and mission and specific tactics for achieving the organization's goals.

- *Organizing:* After managers develop their plans, they have to build an organization that can put these plans into effect. Managers do this by designing organizational structures to execute their plans (often building elaborate organizational charts that divide an organization into divisions, departments, and other parts and designate the people who reside in each position) and by developing systems and processes to direct the allocation of human, financial, and other resources.

- *Leading:* Managers are expected to lead their employees, that is, to motivate them to achieve the organization's goals—quickly and efficiently. Leadership is considered by many to be the most important ingredient for a manager's success. Great leaders can make great things happen, inspiring their employees to do extraordinary things and accomplish extraordinary goals.

- *Controlling:* To accomplish their goals and the goals of the organization, managers must establish performance standards based on the organization's goals and objectives, measure and report actual performance, compare the two, and take corrective or preventive action as necessary.

While these classic functions are still valid, they do not tell the entire story. Managers and workers are entering into a new kind of partnership that is forming the basis of a new reality in the workplace. Today's managers are discovering that they cannot *command* an employee's best work; they can, however, create an environment that encourages employees to want to do their best work. And workers are discovering that, if they expect to survive the constant waves of change sweeping across businesses of all types, they have to find ways to contribute in their organizations in ways that they have never before been called on to do.

The *new functions* of management that tap into the potential of all employees are:

- *Energize:* Today's managers are masters of making things happen. The best managers create far more energy than they consume. Successful managers create compelling visions—visions that inspire employees to bring out their very best performance—and they encourage their employees to act on these visions.
- *Empower:* Empowering employees doesn't mean that you stop managing. Empowering employees means giving them the tools and the authority to do great work. Effective management is the leveraging of the efforts of your team to a common purpose. When you let your employees do their jobs, you unleash their creativity and commitment.
- *Support:* Today's managers need to be coaches, counselors, and colleagues instead of watchdogs or executioners. The key to developing a supportive environment is the establishment of a climate of open communication throughout the organization. Employees must be

able to express their concerns—truthfully and completely—without fear of retribution. Similarly, employees must be able to make honest mistakes and be encouraged to learn from those mistakes.

- *Communicate:* Communication is the lifeblood of every organization. Information is power, and, as the speed of business continues to accelerate, information—the *right* information—must be communicated to employees faster than ever. Constant change and increasing turbulence in the business environment necessitate *more* communication, not *less*—information that helps employees better do their jobs, information on changes that can impact their jobs, and information on opportunities and needs within the organization.

Master these new functions of management, and you'll find that your employees will respond with increased engagement in their work, improved morale and loyalty, and enhanced productivity. The result is better products and services, happier customers, and a more favorable bottom line. Aren't these all things that you would like to see?

ENERGIZING EMPLOYEES

Wouldn't it be great if you could get the very best from your employees each and every day? Well, we have some good news for you: You *can* get the very best from your employees every day of the week. But you can't do it by mandating that your employees give their very best from this day forward, with the occasional pep rally or morale-building meeting, or by threats or coercion. The secret to making this happen is *energizing* your employees—unleashing the passion and talent that resides deep within them.

What can managers do to help unleash the passion and talent in their employees, in short, to energize them? Here are some suggestions:

- Develop a clear vision for where you want the organization to go, and then be sure to communicate the vision widely and often.

ASK BOB AND PETER: What is the Japanese management style that I've heard about?

Briefly, the core of what is known as the Japanese style of management comes from an emphasis in Japanese society on building consensus in group decision making. In Japanese business (as in Japanese society), the group comes before the individual. Managers are, therefore, expected not to command employees but to lead them by consensus. In general, Japanese managers encourage their employees to make suggestions for improvement and to participate in an organization's decision-making process—much more than in most American organizations. They take time to create buy-in, which then allows them to implement decisions much faster after a decision is made. They also tend to favor the development of long-term relationships and strategies over short-term gain. In his book, *Theory Z: How American Business Can Meet the Japanese Management Challenge* (Reading, MA: Addison-Wesley Publication Company, 1981), William Ouchi noted the following characteristics of Japanese organizations: lifetime employment (this has become difficult for many Japanese companies in recent years), slow employee evaluation and promotion, nonspecialized career paths, implicit control mechanisms, collective decision making, collective responsibility, and holistic concern for the employee as a person. To learn more about this approach to management, pick up a copy of Ouchi's book, or visit the Japanese Management Today web site at www.apmforum.com/japan/jmt.htm.

- Ask for and listen to your employees' ideas and suggestions, and, whenever possible, engage them in the process of implementing those ideas and suggestions.
- Be sensitive to your employees' needs at work, and ensure that the work environment is conducive to your employees doing their best work.

- Don't be a prisoner to your office; be sure to regularly visit the people who work for you on their turf and to encourage and inspire them.
- Be honest and truthful with your employees at all times; don't sugarcoat the truth in an attempt to soften the blow of difficult news.
- When you make a promise, be sure to keep it. At the same time, be sure that you don't make promises that you can't keep.

What are you doing to energize your employees? Do you really know what your employees want? Are you responding to your employees' needs, or are you putting them on the back burner—either deferring these decisions until later or hoping they go away altogether? Remember, employees are your most important resource—a resource that is much more productive when it is energized.

EMPOWERING EMPLOYEES

The best (and the most effective) managers realize that they can get far more done—and get it done better, faster, and more cost effectively—by assigning their employees responsibility for accomplishing important tasks and goals, while providing them with the authority that they need to carry out those tasks and goals. It's not enough to assign a goal—employees must also be empowered to accomplish it. Here are some simple approaches to empowering your employees:

- *Put power in the hands of the people doing the work.* The employees closest to customers are in the best position to know what customers really need and, therefore, are in the best position to make decisions that have a direct impact on their customers.
- *Encourage individual responsibility for their contributions.* The flip side of putting power in the hands of the people doing the work is requiring employees to take responsibility for the quality of their work. When employees are trusted to play an active role in

their organization's leadership, they'll naturally respond by taking a personal interest in the quality of their work.

- *Create clarity of roles.* Before employees can be comfortable and effectively share leadership duties with others, they first have to be given clearly defined roles so that they know exactly what they are responsible for, as well as what others are responsible for.

- *Share and rotate leadership.* By moving people in and out of positions of leadership—depending on their particular talents and interests—you can tap the leadership potential that resides within every employee, particularly those employees who aren't a part of the organization's formal leadership hierarchy.

- *Seek consensus (and build creative systems that favor consensus).* One of the best ways to involve others in the leadership process is to invite them to play a real and important role in the discussions and debates that lead to making important organizational decisions. Seeking consensus requires time and a high level of participation and trust, and it results in better decisions that are more easily implemented.

SUPPORTING EMPLOYEES

While it's important to empower your employees—to give them responsibility to accomplish specific organizational tasks and goals along with the authority they need to accomplish them—it's not enough to simply make such assignments and then walk away. The best managers support their employees and act as continuing resources to help guide them on their way. If you don't provide your employees with the support they need, they may decide you don't care—lowering their trust and respect for you—and they may very well engage in activities that are counterproductive to what the organization hopes to achieve.

Here are a number of ways that you can and should support your employees:

ASK BOB AND PETER: What are the best ways for managers to improve communication in an organization?

There are two key aspects to improving communication in any organization. First, you must remove the barriers to communication. What are some common barriers? An "us" versus "them" mentality separating workers from management, an overly formal or strict hierarchy that discourages employees from bringing their ideas or opinions to the attention of management, and an environment of fear that causes workers to be afraid to try new things are just a few possibilities. Take a close look at your own organization and see which ones you find. Second, you must encourage communication within your organization in every way possible. Require your managers to communicate with their staff in a variety of different ways to let them know what's going on. Be real at all times and deal with things as they come up. Invite regular workers to attend management meetings. Encourage managers to meet informally with workers over breakfast or lunch. Ask employees to make their opinions and suggestions for improvement known—and reward them when they do. Launch cross-functional teams of employees—from all levels of the organization—to work together to solve problems. If you take this two-step approach, you'll go a long way toward improving communication in your organization.

- *Have frequent, personal contact with each of your employees.* Your employees won't feel that they have your support if you don't interact with them on a frequent basis. Some employees need more interaction than others, so it's your job to determine how much to provide, to whom, and how often.
- *Recognize the true potential of your employees.* Take time to assess and help further develop your employees' skills and interests, hopes, and dreams while correcting any shortfalls that they may

have. Help employees plan pathways to success within the organization, giving them personal goals that they can strive for.

- *Act on employee ideas and suggestions.* It's one thing to ask employees for their ideas and suggestions; it's another thing altogether to put those ideas and suggestions to use in your organization. Doing so not only can make your organization more effective, but also clearly demonstrates your support to your employees—a message that they will hear loud and clear.

- *Take time to ask employees what they really think about their jobs and about the leadership they receive from you and other managers.* Learning that employees are unhappy in their jobs or with their management team is of little use after an employee quits to take a job with another employer. It is critically important to get candid feedback from employees about their jobs and then to act on it whenever it is in the best interests of the organization.

- *Respect your employees, and treat them as valuable members of your team.* Employees know when you don't respect them or consider their opinions to be of value to the organization, and they will act accordingly when confronted with that realization—becoming demoralized, lowering their productivity, and perhaps even working against the goals of their employer.

- *Involve employees in making decisions that directly affect them.* While not every decision should involve every employee, you'll get far better buy-in and engagement when you give employees the opportunity to have an impact on decisions that directly affect them—improving the ultimate result and your bottom line.

Studies show that the one person who has the most influence on an employee is his or her boss. One of the main reasons talented employees leave organizations is that they feel they are not being supported by their managers. Don't allow this to become the reason that talented employees decide to leave your organization.

COMMUNICATING WITH EMPLOYEES

If there's one place where a great number of managers fail, it's in the area of communication. They don't set up effective communications systems and processes in their organizations; they don't encourage (or demand) their employees to communicate better with one another; and they themselves are ineffective communicators. But, in today's business-at-the-speed-of-light environment, good communication is not just something nice to have—it is absolutely essential.

Are you an effective communicator within your organization? Here are some ways to improve your communications:

- *Regularly inform management of your employees' real feelings, opinions, and ideas about important organizational issues.* Managers must have the best information possible when making decisions—flawed information often results in flawed decisions. This means communicating the real feelings, opinions, and ideas of your employees to your own managers—providing them with information that is not colored by your own biases.
- *Involve* all *of your employees in the decision-making process.* While it may be easier for managers to make decisions themselves—particularly decisions that have the greatest impact on an organization—better decisions often result when you involve all of your employees in the process. Ask for their input and use as much of it as you can.
- *Avoid blaming others when you have to give bad news to your employees.* How many times have you heard a manager say something like, "I fought against this new policy, but it was out of my hands," only to later find out that he or she really didn't fight the decision but simply went along with it? It happens all the time. Instead of passing the buck, managers should be brave enough to honestly make their own views known—even if they just go along with what their managers decide.

THE REAL WORLD

John Lennon once reportedly said: "Life is what you do when you're making other plans." The same can be said of managing. Most every manager can share stories of a well-planned day or week that became completely consumed by a crisis of some sort— a glitch in production, a complaint by a key customer, an employee's personal problem, to name just a few. Good managers know the importance of being flexible and focusing on those things that have to get done. At the same time, they try to learn from what happened to help prevent the same problem from recurring needlessly. This is a dance that must be learned: Keep at those things that *need* to be done while handling those things that *have* to be done, all while maintaining your sanity in the process!

- *When dealing with a difficult situation, have a face-to-face discussion instead of sending a memo or e-mail message or leaving a voice mail message.* Sending someone a written note or message or leaving a voice mail message is a far less personal way of communicating than simply speaking with someone face to face, and it often results in misunderstandings on the part of the person who receives the message. In difficult situations, face-to-face communication requires courage on the part of the manager, but it will result in better communication.

- *Do not let your own opinions and points of view interfere with hearing what someone else is saying.* It's natural for managers to allow their opinions about others—the way they speak, look, or dress, or their reputation in the organization—to create biases that get in the way of communication. While it's easier said than done (but no less important), it is important for managers to neutralize such biases and to be completely open to what their employees say.

- *Go out of your way to make employees comfortable in approaching and speaking with you.* It may be difficult for employees—especially low-status employees—to build up the courage to approach their bosses, much less to tell them what's really on their minds. Make a point of encouraging your employees to approach you with their ideas, issues, and problems, and reward them by thanking them when they do.
- *Do not spend too much—or too little—time worrying about your organization's rumor mill.* Every organization has both formal and informal communication systems. The rumor mill or grapevine, as it is sometimes called, is an important way for employees to communicate informally within organizations. As such, the rumor mill contains valuable information for managers, as well as no small amount of distorted or false information. Managers can keep their finger on the pulse of the organization by monitoring the rumor mill and should make a point of correcting false or distorted information whenever it is detected.

So, how did you do? If you have work to do in the communication department, we have good news for you—it's the focus of Chapter 12 of this book.

─────────────── **POP QUIZ!** ───────────────

Being a manager today requires more than a casual acquaintance with human behavior and how to create an environment that will encourage and allow your employees to give their very best at all times. Reflect for a few moments on what you have learned in this chapter; then ask yourself the following questions:

1. Does your personal style of management incorporate more of the classic functions of managers or more of the new functions of managers? In what ways?

2. What do you do to energize your employees (or sap their enthusiasm)? Are you the type of manager *you'd* like to work for?

3. Would your employees say that they are empowered? If not, what could you personally do to change their answer?

4. In what visible ways do you support your employees? Would your employees agree with your response? Why or why not?

5. Do you communicate openly and honestly with your employees? If not, what do you hide from them, and why? Remember, they can't read your mind, and you don't want them to have to try!

CHAPTER 2

The Challenge of Change

IT'S A NEW WORLD OUT THERE . . .

Change and . . .

How it can impact your organization, employees, and customers.

Understanding the nature of change on the job and your role in it.

Energizing employees and unleashing their potential.

Dealing with change.

Signs of resistance to change and how to get past these roadblocks.

Leading your team through a crisis.

CHANGE HAPPENS

Take a look at any list of new business books, and you're sure to see more than a few on the topic of change and how to deal with it. It's a simple fact of life that change is all around us. If there's one thing you can count on, it's that whatever business environment you're living in today (your customers' preferences, the names and nature of the competition, industry changes, access to resources, etc.) will be different tomorrow—sometimes in small ways, but often in significant ways.

Because the business environment is constantly changing, managers are increasingly expected not only to foresee these new conditions well in advance of their arrival but also to deal with them effectively when they arrive. Change puts a lot of weighty expectations—and pressure—on those in charge. While throughout most of the twentieth century, companies (and the managers who ran them) were rewarded for their conservatism and their resistance to change (large corporations such as General Motors, American Telephone & Telegraph [AT&T], and Sears Roebuck & Company were fortified islands built to stand up to even the largest waves of change), this is no longer the case. To survive, organizations can't ignore change and they cannot fight it. To survive—indeed, to thrive—organizations must anticipate change, prepare for it, and embrace it when it arrives.

And guess whose job it is to anticipate change, prepare for it, and embrace it? You. The manager.

THE FOUR PHASES OF DEALING WITH CHANGE

Change happens—there's nothing you can do to stop it or slow it down. While you can choose to ignore change or refuse to respond to it when

THE BIG PICTURE

GEORGE DAVID

Chairman and CEO, United Technologies Corporation

Question: What are some of the changes you've seen in business over the years?

Answer: A major change—especially in the last half-dozen years—is the impact of what I call the process revolution. And what we find is that revolutionary goals do work. When I was younger, the whole name of the game was the annual business plan negotiation with the parent company. All the divisions wanted to pare back the numbers, have the plan come in, and then cruise right past it and get a big bonus. That's the way American business worked for most of the postwar period—an incremental, few percentage points of improvement each year. What we've learned with the impact of the process revolution in the 1990s is that you can set and achieve revolutionary goals—breathtaking kinds of numbers. I can give you countless examples in the business world where you set a goal for, like, 100 percent improvement and doubling profit or halving cost and it actually happens.

Question: How do you effect revolutionary change like that?

Answer: I sometimes say that the first line of my job description is sales, and that's what I actually do every day, all day. And whether I'm selling stock to investors, products to customers, employment to young people, or new ideas to existing employees, it's all the same thing: I'm always doing sales. And what you look for, benchmarks, are a really good way to sell. That is, when you can see where you are today as compared to somebody else who is there, that's a very effective means of selling. When you have a hard discipline, like the process revolution, you can sell that effectively as well. I spend a lot of my life looking for gee-whiz examples—things that are real and persuasive—that people can buy into and say, "Okay, I believe that." It's much better than the sloganeering that you get sometimes, the motivational talk like we've got to try harder and so forth—stuff that's absolutely useless, and, in fact, it reminds me of all my time going through the former Soviet Union. You look at all these slogans plastered all across the walls of these Soviet factories. Work harder, work better, work smarter, do this, try harder. And the answer, of course, is that it doesn't work. I mean, try harder is not normally an effective means of improvement. What does actually work is having a specific discipline, and I spend a lot of my time with United Technologies Corporation (UTC) people trying to persuade people about the specific disciplines.

Question: What kinds of disciplines?

Answer: We've been through something called lean manufacturing, the Toyota production method, which is basically cellular manufacturing—things like the quality revolution. It's breathtaking what's happened. The way American quality was assured in the postwar period was what I call end-of-line inspection because we built a product, or a car, or an air conditioner and we got it to the end of the line and we turned it on and we drove it, we ran it, and it worked or it didn't work. And if it didn't work, it went to a repair shop for rework and got shipped later on. The Japanese quality revolution is extremely simple in its basic conception because instead of doing end-of-line inspect, the idea is individual process control—at each individual workstation by each individual production employee. And it's the whole notion of you build a perfect product in the first place—that's how you get the right answer. That is, you don't inspect quality at the end—that's the old American way. Instead, you build it perfect in the first place, by the individual employee self-controlling his or her own individual process. And you can make people see that. You show them little techniques that actually make that happen on a shop floor. And you take people and you show them what people sometimes call visual factory, and when someone has seen the visual factory and suddenly understands how this whole thing works, they go out of there with their eyes as big as saucers. And they believe. That's how you do a revolution—first, using benchmarks and showing that you are ahead or behind and, second, applying hard discipline. People need to know what they need to do and not to be sort of motivated with slogans in the old Soviet style.

it arrives (choices that may ultimately have a very negative impact on your career as a manager), this doesn't have any effect whatsoever on its arrival. Change *will* come no matter what you do.

Everyone deals with change in his or her own unique way, but most people go through these four major phases when they are first confronted with change:

1. *Deny change.* The most common initial reaction to change is to deny that it exists. Consider the manager who refuses to cut costs (including redeploying or laying off excess workers) to ensure that the products manufactured by his or her company are priced competitively with the flood of similar products from China. Although the writing is on the wall—in big, bold letters—this manager refuses to see it, putting the company at risk as consumers turn to the imported products, which provide much the same level of quality for significantly less money. The manager should move on to the next phase of dealing with change before he or she does irreparable harm.

2. *Resist change.* Eventually, after denying that change has arrived, in the next phase of dealing with change, people decide to acknowledge its presence but to resist it nonetheless (perhaps hoping that if it is resisted long enough or vigorously enough, it will simply go away, although it never does). If you hear yourself saying things like, "Let's wait a while longer to see what happens before we make a move," or "If it isn't broken, why fix it?" then you can be certain that you're resisting the changes that have arrived on your doorstep.

3. *Explore change.* After resisting change—unsuccessfully—most people begin to realize that they aren't going to be able to stop it, so they slowly begin to explore it instead. This is where managers decide to conduct a study on the suggested change, have a meeting about it, or initiate a pilot program to get a feel for the impact of particular changes—on a temporary, nonbinding basis. There's still

no commitment to accepting the change, but people are definitely warming up to it.

4. *Accept change.* The final phase of change is acceptance. Instead of ignoring or fighting the change that has arrived, the change has been fully accepted and integrated into an organization's thinking, processes, and perhaps even its values. Managers and employees alike have embraced the change and are now on the lookout for the next changes in the organization's environment.

The next time a significant change approaches your business environment, try to become aware of what phase you and your associates and colleagues are in. Are you denying the change? Resisting it? Or exploring and accepting it? Understanding where you are in the four phases of dealing with change can help you get to the final phase more quickly.

DEALING WITH CHANGE AT THE MICRO LEVEL

Is it just us, or does work seem to be busier and more urgent than ever before? It's not like there have never been crises or rush jobs or deadlines in the past—there have been—it's just that the amount of quiet time that allows us to recharge our batteries for the next onslaught of craziness seems to be on a dramatically downward swing.

While as a manager, your job is to keep an eye out for long-term changes looming on the horizon, it's the short-term, day-to-day changes that threaten to take the heaviest toll on your overall health and well-being—both physical and mental. Plans change at a moment's notice, meetings get rescheduled, new product rollouts are accelerated—or slowed down—budgets get slashed, and employees quit and are gone. If there's one thing you can count on in business today, it's that tomorrow everything will be different.

The simple fact is that change happens, and you can't do anything about it. As mentioned in the previous section, you can try to deny it, ignore it, hide it, and pretend it doesn't exist, but that doesn't change the fact that change has arrived. It simply delays the responses that are necessary to deal with it and eventually allow it to become a part of your organization's status quo. Despite this, most managers seem to spend their entire careers trying to fight change. We can only ask this simple question: Why? Without change, organizations would not progress, they would not have an opportunity to serve new customers and take advantage of new markets, and employees would not be able to move forward in their careers. Change allows all this and much more.

We asked Bill Taylor, owner of Lark in the Morning, a musical instrument retailer, how he discusses change with his employees. In his mind, discussing change is like swinging back and forth on a trapeze in the darkness:

> You have a good grip. You get some confidence and maybe even do a pike or hang by your ankles. It begins to feel really good and really comfortable. Then, off in the darkness, you see another trapeze bar swinging toward you, and you get that old familiar feeling in your stomach. You have to completely let go of this trapeze, fly through the air, and grab the next trapeze. You've done this before. You know you can do it again. But it always creates anxiety and uncertainty, maybe even a sense of dread. So you let go, and start flying through the air. And what you have to remember is that the very uncomfortable place in midair is the only place where personal growth occurs. Maybe you don't get comfortable with being in the air, but at least you recognize the value it adds to your life. When you grab the new trapeze, personal growth is over.

SEVEN WARNING SIGNS THAT YOU'RE FIGHTING CHANGE

Are you fighting change in your organization, or are you embracing it? Unfortunately, while you may think you're pretty open to change and perhaps even welcoming its arrival, you may be deep down inside a change fighter. If you're not sure which side of the fence you're on or if you are absolutely certain that you're a change lover instead of a fighter (and you wonder why everyone else seems to think the opposite of you), then be sure to be on the lookout for these seven warning signs of resistance to change:

Warning sign 1: You're playing a new game with the old rules. As games change, you've got to learn the new rules; otherwise, you are bound to lose. As change washes over your organization, you are indeed playing a new game—a game in which the old rules are about as relevant as last week's losing lottery numbers. If you find yourself playing the new game with the old rules, that's one sure sign that you are resisting change in your organization.

Warning sign 2: You're avoiding new assignments. Most people welcome new job assignments, especially when they help lead to new challenges, new opportunities and accomplishments, and perhaps even promotions and pay increases. If you find yourself hiding out when the new assignments are made, however, this is a sign that you have decided that you much prefer the comfort of the status quo to the adventure that is part and parcel with change.

Warning sign 3: You're gumming up the works. Paralysis by analysis is a term used when a manager spends far too much time analyzing every possible angle in making a business decision, often bringing the organization to a grinding halt as it awaits the results of all this study. While a certain amount of analysis is required to make informed decisions, today's fast-changing global business environment might not wait around for you to make a decision that takes too long. If you're slowing down the decision-making process in your organization to a snail's pace, there's a good chance that you've become someone who is resisting change rather than embracing it.

Warning sign 4: You're attempting to control the uncontrollable. Some things just can't be controlled. You can't make the value of your company's stock go up when the markets have decided it's time to go down. You can't prevent a tornado from tearing up the railroad tracks into your plant in Topeka, Kansas. You can't stop your competition from introducing a new series of products specifically designed to steal your key customers. If you're trying to control the uncontrollable, you are not only wasting your time and energy—time and energy that would be better spent on dealing with the effects of such changes—but also clearly resisting the changes in your business environment that are not only unavoidable, but inevitable.

Warning sign 5: You've become a victim of change. There is perhaps no sadder sign that you're resisting change than becoming a victim of it. Instead of embarking on the arduous path of dealing with change and figuring out how to use it to make your organization's products and services more responsive to your customers' needs, you take the easy road, stubbing your toe along the way and ultimately sitting out the change altogether. Sitting on the sidelines nursing your wounds might be a comfortable place to be, but you can be sure that everyone else will eventually pass you by.

Warning sign 6: You're waiting for someone else to step up to the plate. Do you find yourself dragging your feet, hoping deep down inside that someone else will jump in and take charge—perhaps another manager, your boss, or even a competitor? Remember, waiting does not make change go away; it only delays an organization's response to it. This delay can give the competition the leg up it needs to pull ahead of your organization in the marketplace.

Warning sign 7: You've become paralyzed. In its ultimate form, resistance to change results in paralysis; that is, the manager affected by it cannot make decisions or lead initiatives in response to change. The result? Utter failure. Your job as a manager is to make things happen. When you can no longer make things happen, then you have outlived your usefulness as a manager, and you become expendable—not exactly the place most employees in today's leaner organizations want to be.

What can you do when you find that you are exhibiting one or more of these seven warning signs of resistance to change? Become a change leader; that is, proactively lead change in your organization instead of resisting it. Here are some ideas for how to do that:

- *Embrace the change.* Instead of avoiding the change or pretending it doesn't exist, deal with it—head on.
- *Be flexible.* Changes are occurring with increasing frequency in today's fast and furious global business environment. This requires managers to be more flexible than ever in anticipating change and then dealing with it.
- *Be a model.* Employees look to you to show them the behaviors that they should emulate. If you are a change leader instead of a change resister, they, too, will embrace change and use it to their own advantage.
- *Focus.* But be sure to focus on what you *can* do, not on what you *can't* do.
- *Recognize and reward.* You get what you reward. If you reward employees for embracing change, they will do more of that behavior.

The warning signs are just that—warning signs. If they have become a part of your working life, it's not too late to do something about it. Learn to embrace change and to become a change leader. Your organization will thrive as a result, and your employees will become part of a vital workplace that is really getting things done. The result is bound to be good for the bottom line and for your own career—two outcomes that any manager would welcome any day of the week.

WHEN CHANGE BECOMES CRISIS

Change can be a very subtle but powerful force. Like a glacier slowly meandering its way across the face of an alpine mountain slope—moving just a few feet a year—much change in business occurs at a pace

?

ASK BOB AND PETER: I was recently promoted to a supervisory position at a small community college. I will be supervising former coworkers. Are there any web sites where I can pick up hints or tips on how to manage our department efficiently? This is my first position as a supervisor, and I will be receiving training in a few months but for now I am on my own. My first idea is not to change anything because things were running just fine when I accepted the position. If it ain't broke, don't fix it. Do you agree with that as a beginning plan?

Congratulations on your new position! We agree that you should take some time to get your bearings before you change anything in your department. Spend lots of time listening to your staff and getting to know their successes, needs, and problems. After you have a chance to get a good look around, you may then decide whether to make changes. Insert the words *management* or *managing* into your favorite Internet search engine (we prefer google.com), and you'll come up with thousands of sites to peruse in your spare time. However, the quality of these sites varies considerably. Two of the best sites are the sites run by *FastCompany* magazine (http://www.fastcompany.com) and *Inc.* magazine (http://www.inc.com). Both are loaded with huge archives of articles on how to manage effectively. *FastCompany* specializes in being on the cutting edge of management—aiming itself toward today's companies that are ever striving to create products and services faster, cheaper, and better. *Inc.* specializes in small businesses and in all the issues that small business owners and managers encounter as they grow their operations. You might also take a peek at our book *Managing For Dummies* (Hoboken, NJ: Wiley, 2003)—it's chock-full of information that is essential to any new manager.

that is almost imperceptible to those who experience it. But there is another kind of change—crisis—that happens all of a sudden, is often unpredictable, and has the greatest chance of throwing your organization's best-laid plans into disarray and your employees into a state of frenzy.

Such was the case with the September 11, 2001, tragedy, which—in the course of just a few minutes—threw entire companies and, indeed, the American economy itself into crisis for months or even years. Natural disasters such as hurricanes, tornados, and earthquakes can create crises that damage organizations, as can illness, strikes, sharp price increases in production resources (e.g., the price of gasoline, energy, or steel), unexpected drops in consumer demand, and many others. While organizations can be prepared for such crises—and they should have plans in place to deal with them—for the most part, they are unavoidable.

But there is an entirely different set of crises—ones that are avoidable—that can also damage an organization. These are the kinds of crises that you as a manager will confront on an almost daily basis (in direct proportion to the number of direct reports you have and the complexity of your organization and its products or services) and that you must deal with immediately as they arise. Consider these kinds of avoidable crises (and what you as a manager would do to avoid them or deal with them when they arrive):

- Your sales manager, who has perhaps been spending a little too much time on the golf course and not enough time keeping an eye on his staff, doesn't notice that one of his salespeople has begun to insult and berate some of the company's best and most loyal customers. This situation does not become apparent to you until you are called into the CEO's office to explain why these customers have threatened to take their business elsewhere.
- After being passed over for promotion three times with no explanation from management, a key employee (who, coincidentally, is

loved by your major customer's buyers) announces her resignation, effective immediately.

- Afraid that he will be punished for making a mistake, an employee working on the assembly line in a high-volume manufacturing facility ignores a "minor" production flaw in one of your key products. This flaw goes unnoticed for weeks until customers start rejecting shipments of the product and demanding immediate replacement—costing your company millions.

Whatever the source or the nature of the crisis—whether it is avoidable or not—the fact is that as a manager, you will be expected to deal with it. This means being flexible, being smart, and working hard. But, above all, it means being prepared for the most typical crises that can hit your organization—through written plans and procedures—and then taking on the crisis sooner rather than later.

If you don't have a plan or procedure in place to deal with a particular crisis, what then? Our advice is to be fast and flexible, to rely on the advice and input of your associates and colleagues, and to do whatever it takes to deal with the matters at hand. This is no time to start a three-day weekend, to let everyone go home early, or to put off a meeting to deal with the crisis until next week. It's time to roll up your sleeves and get to work—now!

Last, as a manager, you have significant control over avoidable crises and, ultimately, the impact that they have on your organization. If you ignore problems that seem insignificant today, they can blossom into the mother of all crises literally overnight. Keep a close eye on what's going on in your organization, your industry, and your overall business environment. If you have unhappy employees, persistent manufacturing flaws, complaining customers, or changes in your industry that threaten to drive clients to new products and suppliers, then it's in your interest (and vital for your organization's long-term health and well-being) to deal with issues like these as they arise and not wait until they become full-blown crises.

THE REAL WORLD

Some people say the more things change, the more they stay the same. That is, we are fast becoming an age in which the norm *is* change, and, as a result, we must learn how to get things done in a constant state of flux. Waiting until there's time to thoroughly weigh the pros and cons and make a clear, rational decision is increasingly a luxury. Instead, managers must make their best decision based on limited information within tight time constraints. The best managers make assessments quickly with the best available data and then live with their decisions. The worst are timid and struggle with coming to a decision and then almost immediately second-guess themselves, revisiting the decision and often regretting the original conclusions that they made. Strive to be the former type of decision maker.

HELPING EMPLOYEES DEAL WITH CHANGE

As you have seen and experienced in your own organization, change is everywhere, and it directly affects every one of us. Sure, as a manager, you may feel that you are at the epicenter of the change quake, but don't forget that your employees are also affected. And, because they are often even less able to control or have an impact on how the organization deals with change, they may feel more vulnerable to its effects—perhaps even powerless. As a manager, you are in the best position to help your employees weather the changes that they experience on the job. Here are a number of ways to do just that:

- *Be interested in your employees.* Employees appreciate people—especially their managers—who show through their deeds and actions that they really care about them. While you should always show a sincere interest in your employees and in their successes and accomplishments, it is especially important when they are working through the stress and pressures brought about by change. Start with their needs, questions, and issues.

- *Listen.* When employees find themselves undergoing change in their work environments, they want to talk about it—with their coworkers and with their managers. While it's your job to keep your employees apprised of the situation, it's also your job to listen to them. Instead of cutting them off or jumping into the middle of their statements, allow them to vent or fully express their fears or concerns.

- *Seek feedback.* Be sure to seek ideas and feedback on dealing with change from your employees. The best ideas often come from workers on the front lines—the people who work most closely with your customers and the products and services that you sell them—and you should be sure to tap into this important resource.

- *Explain the potential for change.* People do not like to be surprised by change in their jobs or organizations—especially when they are the ones most directly affected—and everyone appreciates being kept informed about potential changes in the environment that might lead to a future crisis. Being informed not only helps employees become better prepared to deal with the coming change but also makes them feel that they are important and valued partners in the organization (which they should be).

- *Don't sugarcoat the truth.* You may think that your employees would much rather hear that everything is going to be okay when it's really not. What your employees want to hear is the truth—what the real problems are, what you're planning to do about them, and how your employees can help get past the coming change—and not some sugarcoated version of it. And when things get really bad, being straightforward and honest with your employees during a crisis will not only help you get through it but also continue to pay dividends in employee goodwill after the crisis has come and gone.

- *Get employees involved.* Giving employees some measure of control over their destiny at work by encouraging them to take part in discussions and decision making will improve their morale while providing you with a valuable source of expertise that you might be hard pressed to find elsewhere.

- *Keep the vision alive.* One of the most important things that leaders do in organizations is to paint a vision for the future. While an organization's vision gives employees something to strive for when things are going smoothly, it is especially important in times of great change when chaos and confusion often reign. When things are at their worst, a compelling vision stands as a shining lighthouse that will both inspire your employees in trying times and guide their efforts toward a common purpose.

POP QUIZ!

A fundamental issue in managing today is managing change in a positive and productive way. After reflecting on this chapter, answer the following questions about change in your life and role as a manager:

1. What is your most common approach to change, and how does that help or hurt you in situations you encounter?
2. What effective strategies have you used when you felt confused or overwhelmed in your life?
3. Have you ever helped a friend or associate who was going through a difficult period? What seemed to be most helpful to him or her?
4. Are there warning signs you could have noticed leading up to a crisis you've experienced? Could you have dealt with things in a way that diverted or minimized the problem?
5. What are three benefits of change that you can get excited about?

PART

II

Leadership: The People Thing

CHAPTER 3

Hiring and Retaining the Very Best People

IT'S A NEW WORLD OUT THERE . . .

Hiring and . . .

How to find (and keep) the very best people.

The hiring process explained.

Where to find the best candidates.

Interview skills demystified.

Picking your best candidate and making an offer.

HIRING (AND KEEPING) GREAT PEOPLE

Finding and hiring the best candidates for a job have never been easy. It's your job, however, to first understand exactly what qualities you're looking for in your new employees, and then to identify them in your job candidates. Here are some of the qualities that most employers look for when hiring new employees:

- *Hard working:* There's nothing that will throw a manager into a paroxysm of rage faster than having an employee who slacks off and who doesn't seem to know the meaning of the words "hard working." Employees who are willing to work hard often go above and beyond the call of duty in serving customers and in attending to the needs of their organizations. As competition in global marketplaces continues to heat up, employees who go above and beyond the call of duty may be the one thing that differentiates organizations that succeed in the long run from organizations that don't.
- *Good attitude:* By "good attitude," we mean people who are positive, friendly, and willing to help customers, clients, and coworkers. As you question potential job candidates, it's important to try to get some idea of what they'll be like to work with for the next 5 or 10 years. Skills are important, but attitude is even more important. As highly successful Southwest Airlines puts it: "Hire for attitude, train for success."
- *Experienced:* Experienced employees are worth their weight in gold. Not only are you more likely to get a better, higher quality work product in less time, but you'll also have someone that is ready to perform at maximum potential in a few days rather than the weeks or months it would take to train someone who is not experienced.

When you interview job candidates, be sure to take the opportunity to ask very pointed questions that require your candidates to demonstrate to you that they can do the job.

- *Go-getter:* This quality is the ability to take initiative to get work done. In an Internet survey that Bob conducted for his book, *1001 Ways to Take Initiative at Work* (New York: Workman, 1999), initiative was ranked as the top reason that employees were able to get ahead where they work (which makes this quality something both you and your potential new hires should be interested in).

- *Team player:* It's almost a cliché that being able to be a team player and to collaborate with others is a critical work skill in today's organizations. But cliché or not, teamwork is necessary to the success of today's organizations and the ability to work well with others is a definite must for employees in any business or industry.

- *Smart:* People who are smart are able to solve problems—and solve them quickly. But keep in mind that, in the world of business, work smarts trump book smarts every time.

- *Responsible:* Employees must take responsibility for their work; employees who constantly try to shift the blame for their problems to other people or other things are employees you cannot afford to employ. Look out for the little things—like showing up for the interview on time—which can be key indicators of your candidates' sense of responsibility.

- *Stable:* Stability is an important quality in the employees you hire; the last thing you want is to hire someone today and then find out that he or she is already looking for the next position tomorrow. Consider how long the job candidate worked with her previous employer and why she left.

So much depends on your identifying and hiring the right people—you can't have a great organization without great people. Far too few managers make this task a priority, instead devoting as little time as

THE BIG PICTURE

CHUCK ROBINSON
Cofounder, M Ship Co.; Member, Nike Board

Question: Why create?

Answer: Being creative is important, and there's no reason to exist if you're not creating. For me, innovating technologically something that has commercial potential is my form of creativity. And if you're not creating, you might as well be six feet under. If you can't leave the world different than you found it, what's the reason for being here? If you're not bound by tradition, you can step back and ask if there is a better way of doing something. I did it in mining, in land transportation, in ocean transportation, and now in boats. It's creating and being willing to do things differently than they've been done before because you feel technologically that there is a way you can improve on the way it's been done before. I had the largest independent mining operation and I had the largest dry cargo shipping operation, which came from nothing. My stockholders put $6 million into developing a mine in Peru. That's all we had to get started. But from February to May of that year, we started shipping iron ore, and by the end of the year, I had generated enough cash to pay back the money that they lent. From that time on, they never put in another penny. And this was all done from nothing. It was leading yourself by your bootstrap but, because I had nothing, I wasn't handicapped by experience. I just did things and I had confidence; when I felt I was right, I had confidence in moving forward.

Question: Do you need employees with special qualifications to be creative?

Answer: No. When I joined the board of Arthur D. Little, in the first board meeting I was told that the greatest asset they had was 1,200 people that had their doctorates. At the time the company was making about $3 or $4 million a year. And I got this long lecture from the

(Continued)

chairman of the board about this great asset—all of these doctorates they had. And I said, "You know, there's something very strange to me about this. You have 1,200 people who have their doctorates, and you pretend to be a commercial operation and you're making $3 to $4 million a year profit. I make $50 to $100 million a year profit and I don't have one doctorate in my organization. I don't understand that." You can have all the intellectual horsepower in the world, but if you don't direct it with imagination and a willingness to take chances and be creative, it doesn't add up to anything.

Question: How important is it to be willing to take risks?

Answer: I had one fellow who graduated from Stanford Business School who worked for me for about five, six, maybe seven years. He moved up in the organization, but I was looking for someone to handle my marketing, so I appointed him vice president in charge of marketing. Another fellow that had been with me longer and who also graduated from Stanford Business School came to me and said, "I'm just terribly shattered by your decision. I've worked for you for x number of years and I think you have to admit that I never made a mistake." I said, "That's the problem. If you've never made a mistake, you've never made a decision on time. If you were a 100 percent certain you're right, you're too late. I want somebody who will be right 80 percent of the time or 90 percent of the time, but who's prepared to fail. You're never prepared to fail. And as a result, you're not moving us forward." He stopped and thought about it and said, "I guess I'll go out and fail at something." I said, "Well, you just failed at getting promoted to vice president. Why don't you think about that?"

they can get away with when it comes to preparing for and conducting interviews. The quality of the results of your hiring process are generally directly proportional to the amount of time that you are willing to sink into it. Put more time into the process, and you'll probably find the people you seek; put less time into the process, and you'll be wondering why you can't find anyone to fill your position.

CREATING A JOB DESCRIPTION

Before you begin the recruiting process, it's important to understand and define the expectations you have for your candidates. When you are clear about the kind of person you're seeking, you'll immediately know it when you find the right candidate for the job. There are generally two recruiting situations: hiring for an entirely new job, or hiring to replace an employee in an existing job. Let's consider each in turn.

If the job is new, you're in luck: This is the perfect time to specify your ideal candidate. Fully describe in the job description all the tasks and responsibilities of the position and the minimum necessary qualifications and experience. Does the job require fluency in HTML? Then say so. Be specific, not vague or fuzzy. Work hard on the job description now and you'll have less work to do when you make the hire.

If you're filling an existing position, then you're also in luck: This is the perfect time to dust off the existing job description and make changes where necessary. Be sure that the job description closely reflects the tasks and requirements of the position. Often, a position's responsibilities will shift over time as duties are added and taken away over a number of years. Unfortunately, job descriptions rarely keep up with this responsibilities creep. Now is the perfect opportunity to update the job description to reflect reality.

Before you start your recruitment effort, create an interview outline using the new or updated job description to outline the most important qualities that you're seeking in your new hire. Seek input from other managers who will interact with the person to be hired to find out what kinds of qualities they would like to see in the position as well. Use the outline you create to guide you in the interview process.

FINDING THE BEST CANDIDATES

The success of your organization depends on you—and others in a position to hire new employees—to find the very best people possible for

ASK BOB AND PETER: What is the most effective way new managers can gain respect and trust from their new team? What challenges do managers have if they are younger than some of their staff?

The most effective way to gain trust and respect is by being there for the team and following through on your promises. Other things are also important—technical skill, experience, personality, work ethic, and more—but you build respect and trust by listening, supporting, and honoring your commitments when you make promises. For example, if you empower a team of employees to study a problem in production and make recommendations, then do everything in your power to implement the team's recommendations quickly. If you don't, you will lose the respect and the trust of your employees—instantly. While some older employees may initially have a problem with having a boss who is younger, if the boss works hard to build respect and trust with his or her employees, in time, this issue will fade.

the job. It's simple: If you're able to hire better people, your business will be better too. Not everyone is meant for every job—some people, no matter how talented they may be, are ill-suited for certain jobs. Imagine what an amazing organization you would have if everyone hired was perfectly suited for their jobs.

Finding the best candidates starts with having a system that helps you track them down. The best candidates can be found anywhere—you really don't know where you might find your next award-winning graphics artist or imaginative welder. Here are some ways to the best find job candidates for your organization:

- *Taking a close look within:* Before you launch a massive search for candidates outside of your organization, take a close look within. If, after you exhaust your internal candidates, no one turns up, then feel free to look outside your organization. Taking a look inside your organization first will make the process faster and less expensive while resulting in employees who are happy that they are being given a leg up on the competition.

- *Personal referrals:* Many companies rely on referrals from current employees for the best candidates when jobs open up. As it turns out, this is not just a coincidence—research shows that people hired as a result of referrals from current employees work out better, stay with the company longer, and are happier. Involve your employees in the recruiting process by asking them to refer their talented friends and relatives.

- *The Internet:* Most companies have discovered the advantages of Web sites in presenting almost unlimited amounts and kinds of information about your firm and about your job openings—in text, audio, graphic, and video formats. Not only is the Internet a great way to get your recruiting information out to a wide, even international audience for minimal cost, but your Web pages are on the job 24 hours a day, 7 days a week.

- *Want ads:* Want ads have long been one of the most commonly used ways of publicizing job openings. On the plus side, they are an easy (if expensive) way to get your message out to a large cross-section of potential candidates—both locally or nationwide. On the minus side of the equation, running a want ad can generate a huge stack of job candidates—many of whom may be completely unqualified for your position.

- *Temporary agencies:* Hiring temps, or temporary employees, has turned into an effective way to hire new employees. When you hire a temp, not only do you get the benefit of his or her services, but if you like the employee's performance, most temp agencies will allow you to hire the employee on a full-time status for a nominal fee or after a minimum time commitment. And what's really great is that if you don't like the temp you're assigned, you can simply call the agency, and they will send a replacement.

- *Employment agencies:* Employment agencies are almost required if you're filling a particularly specialized position or high-level executive, are recruiting in a small market, or simply prefer to outsource the recruiting and screening of your applicants. You'll pay a lot of money for the privilege—one-third of the employee's first-year salary, or more—but you'll probably end up with truly top-notch candidates for your job.

- *Professional associations:* Almost every profession has an association that look out for their interests. Doctors have the American Medical Association, elementary school principals have the National Association of Elementary School Principals. Most associations offer job search services for their members and, if you are looking for candidates with specialized experience related to the association, the association will likely welcome your job listings (which they will generally publish for free on their Web site and in newsletters, and for a nominal fee in journals or magazines).

Be creative when you're looking for someone to fill your job openings. The ideas above are the most common, but they are by no means the only way to find the right candidates for your job.

BECOMING A WORLD-CLASS INTERVIEWER

Once you've narrowed the field down to the top three or five applicants, it's time to interview. But first, a question: What kind of interviewer are you? Are you the kind of interviewer who doesn't even look at the candidates' resumes until five minutes before they walk in the door, or do you take time in advance to "get to know the candidates" in advance, well before they arrive?

If you want to become a world-class interviewer, then you've got to seriously prepare for your interviews. Your best candidates have spent hours preparing for their interviews with your company; don't you think that you should spend at least as much time getting ready for the interview as the men and women whom you're going to interview? (We do.)

Asking the Right Questions

The central focus of the interview process is the questions that you ask your job candidates and the answers that you receive. Asking the best questions gets you the best answers. Ask lousy questions and guess what you get? Lousy answers—answers that won't help you decide whether or not the candidate is going to be right for the job.

Great interviewers ask great questions. According to Richard Nelson Bolles, author of the perennially popular job-hunting guide *What Color Is Your Parachute?* (Berkeley, CA: Ten Speed Press, 2004) you can categorize all interview questions under one of the following four headings:

1. *Why are you here?* Ask yourself: Why is the person sitting across from you going to the trouble of interviewing with you today? You have just one way to find out—ask. While you may assume that the answer is that he or she wants a job with your firm, you may be surprised at what you find.

2. *What can you do for us?* The candidates you meet are all going to try to dazzle you with their remarkable personalities, experience, work ethic, and love of teamwork. But, despite what many job candidates seem to believe, the question is not, "What can your firm do for me?"—the question that you want an answer to is, "What can you do for us?"

3. *What kind of person are you?* There are plenty of angels and demons in your candidate pool. No matter who you hire, you're going to be spending a lot of time with him or her. Hiring someone you'll want to work with over the long haul is essential—for your mental health, as well as the mental health of your colleagues and coworkers. Aside from basic personality, you'll also want to take the time to confirm a few other issues while you're at it: Are your candidates

honest and ethical? Are they responsible and dependable? Can they work independently?

4. *Can we afford you?* Are you prepared to pay what it takes to get the best candidates for your job? Can your company afford it? Remember that salary is but one component of a compensation package. The availability of benefits, a nicer office, or a more impressive title will weigh into a candidate's decision on whether or not to accept a job offer.

Interviewing Do's

Interviewing is an art; here are some ideas on how to paint your masterpiece:

- *Review the resumes of each interviewee the morning before interviews start.* Don't wait to read your interviewees' resumes during the interview, prepare in advance and tailor your questions to the specific qualifications of your candidate.
- *Become intimately familiar with the job description.* Be sure that you are an expert on all the different duties and requirements of the job. Not only will you do a better job interviewing your candidates, but there's less chance that you'll surprise new hires with duties that you didn't tell them about.
- *Draft your questions before the interview.* This is your chance to ask your candidate questions (and receive answers) that will help guide your hiring decision. Make a list of questions before interview starts, then go through your questions one by one as the interview progresses.
- *Select a comfortable environment for both of you.* Avoid distracting your candidate (and you) with an environment that is something less than comfortable. You don't need a heater to make your candidates sweat—they'll do plenty of that anyway as soon as the interview starts.

- *Take lots of notes.* If you're planning to interview more than one candidate, take notes during your discussions. Good notes help you keep track of your thoughts, and they can be an invaluable aid in the event that you or your organization is sued because of an unpopular hiring decision.

Keep asking questions until you're satisfied that you have all the information you need to make your decision. Finally, note your own impressions of the candidates:

- "Top-notch performer—the star of her class."
- "Fantastic experience with developing applications in a client-server environment. The best candidate yet."
- "Where did they dig up *this* candidate?"

Interviewing Don'ts

For every interview "do," there is probably a corresponding interview "don't." Some interviewing don'ts are merely good business. It's not smart, for example, to dwell on questions that have nothing to do with a candidate's suitability for a particular job. Other interviewing don'ts have legal ramifications. For example, although you can ask applicants whether they are able to perform specific job-related tasks (such as lift a 50-pound box) in the United States, you can't ask them whether they are disabled, are married, have a car, and a variety of other questions. In fact, there are some questions that you absolutely should never ask a job candidate. Here's a brief summary of subjects to avoid:

- Race.
- National origin.
- Sex.

- Sexual orientation.
- Marital status.
- Religion (or lack thereof).
- Arrest and conviction record.
- Height and weight.
- Debts.
- Disability.

The good news is that none of these possible subjects relate to the ability of applicants to perform their jobs. You can therefore focus on asking questions that directly relate to the candidates' ability to perform required tasks and avoid those that don't—legal or not.

Five Steps to Better Interviewing

Every interview consists of five key steps:

Step 1: Welcome the applicant. Greet your candidates warmly and chat with them briefly to help them relax. Ask about the weather, the difficulty of finding your offices, or how they found out about your position.

Step 2: Summarize the position. Briefly describe the job, the kind of person you're looking for, and give your candidate a short outline of how the interview process will work.

Step 3: Ask your questions (and then listen). Ask questions relevant to the position and covering the applicant's work experience, education, and other related topics. Spend the majority of your time listening rather than talking; avoid trying to sell the job to an applicant when you should be trying to find out if he or she is a good fit.

Step 4: Probe experience and find out the candidate's strengths and weaknesses. Although it can take some digging to get the real story, the best predictor of future behavior is past behavior. Ask questions that probe your applicants' experience and that require your candidates to name their strengths and weaknesses.

Step 5: Conclude the interview. Give your candidates an opportunity to offer any further information that they feel is necessary for you to make a decision and to ask questions about your firm or about the job. Thank them for their interest, and let them know when they can expect to hear your firm.

THE SELECTION PROCESS

It's time to take the next step in the hiring process—evaluating your candidates and making your selections. You should by now have a strong pool of candidates from which to choose but, before you make your final decision, you should get a little more information first.

Checking References

Believe it or not, a lot of people lie about their experience. In some cases, these lies may take the form of an occasional fudged date or job title while, in other cases, these lies may be major, super-size whoppers, such as the candidate who claims he has a PhD from Harvard but who actually dropped out of the 8th grade.

The point here is that resumes and interviews are great hiring tools, but you'll need to conduct a reference check to confirm whether or not your candidates are who they say they are before you make a hiring decision. In some organizations, you the manager may be expected to do reference checks, while in other organizations the human resources department takes on the responsibility. Whichever the case, conduct an exhaustive background check before you make that offer.

ASK BOB AND PETER: Is there any magic formula for discovering how many support people are needed in a company? I am the office manager for a family business composed of three partners—a father and two sons. There are four managers under the partners. I am responsible for seeing that we are staffed appropriately to "get the work done." I often feel that my staff and I only put fires out instead of really getting everything running well! Any helpful hints?

The answer to your question varies considerably depending on the exact duties that the support people take on. For example, if all the support person is responsible for is typing an occasional document, scheduling meetings, and greeting visitors, then he or she could probably easily support four or five managers or executives. However, if the support person is given more duties and responsibilities—for example, purchasing supplies, handling mail, producing proposals or reports, developing budgets, and so forth—he or she may be able to effectively support only one or two managers or executives. The best rule of thumb is to first try staffing with the least number of support people possible and then assessing the satisfaction of both the managers/executives and the support people. If everyone is screaming or if your support folks aren't able to consistently get quality work done on time, add another support person and reassess.

Here are some tips for conducting reference checks that will get you the information you need to make an informed hiring decision:

- *Check academic references.* The exaggeration of educational experience is a common problem, so you should start your reference check here. If your candidates can't tell the truth about their education, then why would you trust anything else they have to say?

Thank them for applying, but don't even think about hiring these candidates.

- *Call current and former supervisors.* Unfortunately, many businesspeople are rightfully concerned that they may be sued for libel or defamation of character if they say anything negative about current or former subordinates—making it hard to get references from your candidate's current or former supervisors. But try anyway, you never know what you'll find out.

- *Check your network of associates.* It's really a small world after all. In this increasingly interconnected world of business, there's a possibility that one of your friends, relatives, or work associates knows your candidate or knows of him. Put out the word with your network and see what turns up.

- *Do an online search.* Do a Google (www.google.com) search of the candidate's name, perhaps along with the name of the company where he or she last worked or the city in which he or she lives. You might find anything from an article praising her business smarts, to a police mug shot of your candidate. It's worth a quick look.

Reviewing Your Notes

Take time now to review the notes that you took during the course of the interview, along with candidates' resumes and the results of your reference checks. Consider how the candidates compare to the standards that you set for the position. Assign each of your candidates into one of the following categories:

- *Winners:* These people are the best of the best. You're comfortable that any one of them would do a great job.

- *Potential winners:* These candidates aren't as strong as the people in your Winners category, but they are still worth consideration—especially if you can't land one of your top candidates. Before you

THE REAL WORLD

Hiring an employee is far from a perfect science. It's a matter of best guesses and hunches, constantly trying to minimize your risk and improve the chances that an employee will succeed. Making matters worse, most managers tend to hire after their own image, thus multiplying their perceived strengths but also compounding their weaknesses. For example, a big-picture strategist will likely look to hire an analytical person who thinks the same way (and values the same things) as he or she does. What would likely be of greater help, however, is for that manager to hire someone who is different and perhaps even opposite to himself or herself, in this case, someone very detailed and process oriented. In other words, the best managers look to complement their owns skills and strengths—not to enhance those existing capacities.

hire from this pool, however, be sure that any questions you have about their abilities or experience are resolved.

- *Losers:* These candidates are clearly unacceptable, period, case closed. Don't even think about hiring someone in this group.

Conducting a Second (or Third) Round

Is it time to make that job offer to your best candidate? Well, that depends on your organization's policies or culture, or whether you're certain that you've identified the best candidate. If that's the case, you may need to bring candidates in for one or more additional rounds of interviews.

How many rounds and levels of interviews to conduct depends on the nature of the job, the size of your company, and your policies and procedures. If the job is simple or at a relatively low level in your organization, just one short phone interview may be sufficient to determine the best candidate for a job. If the job is complex or at a relatively high level in the organization, however, you may need several rounds of in-person interviews to determine the best candidate.

Rank your candidates within the groups of winners and potential winners that you established during the evaluation phase of the hiring process. Don't waste your time ranking the losers—you won't hire them anyway. Rank the best candidate in your group of winners as first, the next best as second, and so on. When you complete the ranking of your candidates, the best people for the job will be readily apparent.

MAKING AN OFFER

Soon after you make a hiring decision, you'll want to make an employment offer. Don't waste a moment's time—the best candidates are often being pursued by more than one potential employer. Pick up the phone and offer your number one candidate the job. If your first choice doesn't accept the offer in a reasonable amount of time, or if you're at an unbreakable impasse on the details of the offer, then go on to your second choice. Work through your pool of winners until you either make a hire or exhaust the list of candidates.

Here are some tips to keep in mind as you rank your candidates and make your final hiring decision.

Be Objective

For a variety of reasons, we all prefer certain people more than others. Unfortunately, this preference can obscure your job candidates' shortcomings, while a better qualified but less likable, candidate may come out a loser.

Avoid being unduly influenced by your candidates' looks, personalities, hairstyles, or personal dress code. While these characteristics might be nice to look at, they can't tell you how well your candidates will actually perform the job. Stick to the facts—you'll never be 100 percent right every time, but you'll sure be close.

Trust Your Gut

What do you do when you're faced with a decision between two equally qualified candidates? If you have no clear winner, listen to yourself—what is your gut telling you to do? Do you have a feeling that one candidate will do a better job than the other? If so, go with it. While your hiring decisions should be as objective as possible, sometimes you've got to rely on subjective judgments.

In the real world, rarely are two candidates equally qualified. This is where the time you spent reviewing your candidates' paperwork and qualifications before the interview comes in handy. Anything that gives one person an edge over another should be used to help you make your final decision.

Other options include:

- Asking candidates to prepare a strategy paper on how they'd approach the job.
- Giving them each a nonpaid assignment and see how they do.
- Trying them on a paid project.

Until you finally make your hire—and perhaps even for a few weeks beyond—keep in touch with other top candidates. You may be making a call to them when your first choice turns out to be a dud.

--- **POP QUIZ!** ---

Finding and hiring the best employees requires a serious and concerted effort to identify the very best candidates and to separate them from the also-rans. Reflect for a few moments on what you have learned in this chapter; then ask yourself the following questions:

1. What are your strengths and weaknesses in hiring?
2. What is your organization's hiring process? Who does it involve?
3. What can you do to ensure that you find the best candidates to interview?
4. What are essential elements of an effective interview?
5. Are you willing to *not* fill a position if you can't find the "best" candidate?

Motivating Employees

IT'S A NEW WORLD OUT THERE . . .

Motivating employees and . . .

Understanding how to get the best from your employees—every day of the week.

The world's greatest management principle.

Understanding what motivates your employees.

Getting creative with rewards and recognition.

Putting together a system of low-cost rewards.

THE WORLD'S GREATEST MANAGEMENT PRINCIPLE

Wouldn't it be great if all your employees came to work—each and every day of the week—excited about being there, fully engaged, and giving their best efforts? Perhaps you're one of the lucky managers whose employees already fit this description. If so, then keep on doing whatever it is that you're doing. But, if for some reason your employees aren't as excited about their jobs as they could or should be or if they are not fully engaged and giving their best efforts, then you've got a problem. The good news is that this is a problem that you as a manager have a great deal of influence over.

Motivating employees is what it's all about, and, while you can't reach into someone's head and turn on his or her motivation switch, by using rewards and recognition, you *can* create the kinds of conditions that will result in motivated employees.

But before we get into all the details of rewards and recognition, we first need to let you in on a little secret: the *world's greatest management principle*. Now, you may think you already know what this principle is—something along the lines of "He who has the gold rules," or "Do unto others before they do unto you"—but you would be wrong. It's a simple rule that can save you countless hours of frustration and extra work, while saving your organization many thousands, or perhaps even millions, of dollars: *You get what you reward.*

In other words, when you reward certain kinds of behavior— whether it's good or bad for the organization—that's what you'll get more of. For example, let's say that you would like your employees to take more initiative in their jobs and make and implement more suggestions for improvements to company systems and procedures. The way to get more of this kind of behavior is to reward your employees— using anything from simple verbal praise to cash or other financial incentives—whenever they take initiative in their jobs and make and implement suggestions for improvement. It's a simple idea, and it works.

One thing managers have to be particularly careful about is to ensure that they aren't rewarding the *wrong* employee behavior. Consider this common example: It seems that certain employees in every organization are highly productive—getting more work done in less time—while other employees are significantly less productive. A common response by managers to this kind of behavior is to assign more work to the more effective employees, while assigning less work to the less effective employees. While that kind of makes sense on the surface, the manager who does this is actually rewarding low-performing employees (and reinforcing their behavior) by giving them less work. At the same time, high-performing employees are being punished for being high performers when the manager gives them more work—making it less likely that they will continue to be high performers for very long.

Remember: You get what you reward!

WHAT DO YOUR EMPLOYEES WANT?

When it comes to rewards, many managers believe that the only thing that their employees want is more money. However, while money can be an important way of letting employees know their worth to the organization, it tends not to be a sustaining motivational factor to most individuals. That is, cash rewards such as salary, bonuses, and the like are nice, but seldom are they what motivate people to give their best efforts on the job.

Cash rewards have one more problem. In most organizations, performance reviews—and corresponding salary increases—occur only once a year, whereas the things that cause someone to be motivated today—such as being thanked for doing a good job, involved in decision making, and supported by their manager—are typically activities that have happened recently within the immediate work group. To motivate employees, managers need to recognize and reward achievements and progress toward goals by employees on a daily basis.

When you ask employees what employee motivation is most important to them, rarely is money listed first; in fact, in numerous studies we've seen, seldom is money ranked above fifth in performance. What *is* most important to employees are intangibles such as being appreciated for the work they've done, being kept informed about things that affect them, having interesting work, and having a sympathetic manager who takes time to listen to them. These intangibles cost little or nothing to implement, but they do take the time and thoughtfulness of a manager who cares.

ENERGIZING TODAY'S EMPLOYEES

Do you know what your employees want—what motivates them to work harder and to become more efficient and effective? To answer these questions, Bob recently surveyed some 1,500 employees in seven different industries.

The most important things managers can do to develop and maintain motivated, energized employees have no cost, but rather are a function of how employees are treated on a daily basis. The following items—ranked in priority order—are some of the things today's employees indicate are most important to them:

- *Praise—personal, written, electronic, and public:* Although you can thank someone in 10 to 15 seconds, most employees report that they're never thanked for the job they do—especially not by their manager. Systematically start to thank your employees when they do good work, whether one-on-one in person, in the hallway, in a group meeting, on voice mail, in a written thank-you note, on e-mail, or at the end of each day at work. Better yet, go out of your way to act on, share, and amplify good news when it occurs—even if it means interrupting to thank them for a great job they've done. By taking the time to say you noticed and appreciate their efforts, those efforts—and results—will continue.

- *Support and involvement:* How well you provide information employees need to do their jobs, how well you support your employees when they make mistakes, how well you involve employees when making decisions, and whether you ask your employees for their opinions and ideas create the foundation for this item. Employees want more than ever to know how they are doing in their jobs and how the company is doing in its business. Involving employees is both respectful and practical: You increase their commitment and ease in completing the work and implementing changes and new ideas.

- *Autonomy and authority:* Most employees value being given room to do their work as they best see fit. Do you allow employees to decide how best to do their work, give them increased job autonomy and authority, allow them to pursue their ideas, or give them a choice of assignments whenever possible? These elements all allow autonomy and authority to flourish—and provide a powerful motivation to employees. The ultimate form of recognition for many employees is to have increased autonomy and authority to get their job done, including the ability to spend or allocate resources, make decisions, or manage others. Greater autonomy and authority means, "I trust you to act in the best interests of the company, to do so independently, and without the approval of me or others." Increased autonomy and authority should be awarded to employees as a form of recognition itself for the past results they have achieved. Autonomy and authority are privileges, not rights, which should be granted to those employees who have most earned them based on past performance and not based on tenure or seniority.

- *Flexible working hours:* Time is the new currency for today's employees, who expect work to be an integrated part of their lives— not their entire lives. Given that in one recent study some 83 percent of employees reported wanting more time with their families, one way to help accommodate this desire is through greater flexibility of the hours employees work. With technology today, work is increasingly becoming a state of mind rather than a place to be. Consider allowing top performers to leave work early when necessary, have flexible working hours, earn time off from work, and have comp time for extra hours worked. Today's employees value their time and their time off. Be sensitive to their off-schedule needs, whether they involve family or friends, charity or church, education, or hobbies, and provide flexibility whenever you can so they can meet those obligations. Time off may range from an occasional afternoon off to attend a child's play at school or the ability to start the workday an hour early so they can leave an hour early. By allowing work to fit best with employees' life schedule, you increase the chances that they'll be motivated to work harder while they are at work and to do their best to make their schedule work. As long as the job gets done, what difference does it matter what hours they work?

- *Learning and development:* Today's employees highly value learning opportunities in which they can gain skills that can enhance their worth and marketability in their current job as well as future positions. Find out what your employees want to find out, how they want to grow and develop, and where they want to be in five years. Give them opportunities as they arise and the ability to choose work assignments whenever possible. When you give employees choices, more often than not they'll rise to meet or exceed expectations. Do you support and encourage employees to learn new skills, discuss career options with them, allow them to participate in learning activities, and discuss what they've learned after completed projects and assignments?

- *Manager availability and time:* In today's fast-paced world of work in which everyone is expected to get more done faster, an employee's personal time with his or her manager is in itself also a form of recognition. As managers are busier, taking time with employees is even more important. The action says: "Of all the things I have to do, one of the most important is to take time to be with you, the person or persons I most depend on for us to be successful." Especially for younger employees, time spent with their manager is a valued form of validation and inspiration, as well as serving a practical purpose of learning and communication, answering questions, discussing possibilities, or just listening to an employee's ideas, concerns, and opinions. Are you available to address employees' questions and concerns, get to know them, and listen to their nonjob issues? Being accessible to employees—and getting back to them promptly at times when you are not—is critical for building lasting relationships with your employees. Remember, you can't have an open door policy with a closed mind!

ASAP-CUBED

It's odd but true: The most powerful motivators tend to also be the simplest ones with the least cost, starting with praise. When you think of praising an employee, remember this simple approach: ASAP-cubed:

- *As soon:* Timing is very important when using positive reinforcement. Give praise as soon as a desired behavior is displayed.
- *As sincere:* Praise someone because you are truly appreciative and excited about the other person's success. Otherwise, it may come across as a manipulative tactic.
- *As specific:* Avoid generalities in favor of details of the achievement. For example, "You really turned that angry customer around by focusing on what you could do for him, not on what you could not do for him."
- *As personal:* A key to conveying your message is praising in person, face to face. This shows that the activity is important enough to you to put aside everything else you have to do and just focus on the other person.

Ask Bob and Peter: What can you do when the owners of a company just don't believe in rewarding their employees? None of the employees are feeling appreciated for their work. My concern is for the laborers in our warehouse. No one ever says a kind word to them; no one sees how much they need a pat on the back. The owners of the company think that giving a Christmas dinner every year is your reward. Morale is so low right now. How can I present a reward system to the company? How can I make them see what a difference it would make?

You've got to somehow get on management's radar screen. The point is that rewarding employees isn't just a good idea because it makes employees feel better (although that's not such a bad thing, is it?) but that it makes good business sense. Happy employees are more productive, they provide better customer service, and they are less apt to leave a company for other opportunities. A study by Sears Roebuck at 800 of its stores found that if employee attitudes on 10 essential factors (e.g., treatment by bosses and workload) improve by 5 percent, customer satisfaction will jump 1.3 percent—leading to a 0.5 percent increase in revenues. For Sears—with annual revenues of about $41 billion—this translates to more than $200 million in additional revenues a year.

So how do you get on management's radar screen? Try posting an article or survey on the benefits of employee rewards on company bulletin boards. Bob's web site—http://www.nelson-motivation.com—has lots of free articles, interviews, and more on the Resources page, which you can post or pass on to management and coworkers. Give your boss or your boss's boss a copy of Bob's book *1001 Ways to Reward Employees* (New York: Workman, 1994)—it's full of creative and effective ideas for rewarding employees, most of which cost little or nothing to implement—or *The 1001 Rewards & Recognition Fieldbook* (New York: Workman, 2003), which has an entire chapter devoted to the topic of selling recognition to top management.

- *As positive:* Too many managers undercut praise with a concluding note of criticism. When you say something like, "You did a great job on this report, but there were quite a few typos," the "but" becomes a verbal erasure of all that came before.
- *As proactive:* Lead with praising and "catch people doing things right" or else you will tend to be reactive—typically about mistakes—in your interactions with others.

BE CREATIVE WHEN REWARDING EMPLOYEES

Recognition is one of the most powerful activities that a manager can do to increase productivity, improve morale, and provide a sense of meaning on the part of employees on a day-to-day basis. Yet, in most work environments, this activity is underutilized and even randomly applied. Studies indicate that being thanked for doing a good job is one of the most motivating incentives an employee reports receiving, even though some 58 percent of employees say they seldom if ever receive such thanks from their managers where they currently work. When recognition is tied to desired performance, it becomes a big driver of enhancing that performance, both the quantity and quality of individual effort and results.

The value of recognition is almost common sense, but not common practice in most fast-paced business environments today. In fact, one of the obstacles to getting people to provide more recognition is that many managers already think they are doing a good job at recognizing others—even though others may not agree.

When it comes to rewards, most managers feel that the only thing that their employees want is more money. While money can be an important way of letting employees know their worth to the organization, it tends not to be a sustaining motivational factor to most individuals. That is to say, salary raises are nice, but seldom are they what motivates people to do their best on the job.

Another limitation to money as a reward is that, in most organizations, performance reviews—and corresponding salary increases—occur only once a year. To motivate employees, managers need to reward achievements and progress toward goals by employees much more frequently than once a year. Indeed, rewarding performance needs to take place on almost a daily basis. More times than not, what is more important to workers are intangibles such as being appreciated for the work they've done, being kept informed about things that affect them, and having a sympathetic manager who takes time to listen to them. None of these intangibles are very costly, but they all do take the time and thoughtfulness of a manager who cares.

How then can a manager provide rewards that are more frequent and personal? The answer is simple: Be creative. Take time to find out what specifically motivates and excites each of your employees, and then see what you can do to make those things happen.

When one of your employees has put in extra effort on a key project or achieved a goal you had mutually set, immediately recognize the achievement fittingly in a unique, memorable way. You will find that the more creative and unique you are with the reward, the more fun it will be for the employee, yourself, and others in the organization, for example:

- Have a discussion with your employee about his or her work preferences and ambitions and how you might help with each.
- Write a letter to the employee's family telling them about the recent accomplishment of the employee and what it means to you and the company.
- Arrange for a top manager in your company to have a recognition lunch with the employee, or have the president call the employee to personally thank him or her for a job well done.
- Find out what an employee's personal hobby is, and purchase a small gift that relates to that hobby.

- Wash an employee's car in the parking lot during lunch one day.
- Make lunch or dinner for a small group of high performers.

These ideas—and hundreds of others like them—are limited only by your imagination, time, and creativity. Such rewards will not only uniquely single out exceptional employees but also create positive stories that they will tell to others time and time again. Friends, family, and coworkers will get to hear about the individual's achievement and what the company did to celebrate it, and the employee will get to relive the recognition many times.

You can even work recognition mechanisms into your company's operations. For example, in some companies managers take time to let employees publicly thank others in the company who went out of their way to help them or even ask if anyone has a public praise they want to share. They make it a priority to write simple thank-you notes when employees do good work. They present traveling trophies to individuals who modeled the organization's core values such as customer service or teamwork. They use internal publications to highlight successes of the organization, individuals, or teams.

Rewarding employees for exceptional work they've done is critical to keeping them motivated to continue to do their best. Although money is important, you can potentially get even more benefit from personal, creative, and fun forms of recognition. Try such rewards for yourself to see the pride, enthusiasm, fun—and motivation—that can be generated.

THE LEGEND OF THE FLOPPY CHICKEN

The Floppy Chicken Award was created by former KFC chief executive officer David Novak (now chairman of Yum! Brands, parent company of KFC, Pizza Hut, A&W, Long John Silver's, and Taco Bell) to recognize employees who go the extra mile. Novak personally presents the numbered floppy chicken to the recipient, along with a handwritten note of personal thanks and a $100 gift certificate. A photo of the presentation is put on permanent display in the Walk of Leaders, which is located in a prominent area of KFC's corporate headquarters.

KFC's Random Acts of Recognition program is a peer recognition program designed to encourage employees to recognize coworkers who "walk the talk" (defined as following the company's eight leadership principles) while having fun doing it. Twice a month, an employee marching band parades through corporate headquarters and presents a bucket of balloons (in a KFC chicken bucket, of course) to a lucky recipient who walks the talk.

PUTTING TOGETHER A SYSTEM OF
LOW-COST REWARDS

As we mentioned earlier, the best rewards are thought out and planned. While spontaneous, spur-of-the-moment rewards are an important item in any manager's motivational toolbox (and are to be encouraged because of their immediacy and sincerity), take time to put together a system of low-cost rewards in your organization that include the following characteristics:

- *Link rewards to organizational goals.* To be effective, rewards need to reinforce the behavior that leads to an organization's goals. Use rewards to increase the frequency of desired behavior and decrease the frequency of undesired behavior.
- *Define parameters and mechanics.* After you identify the behaviors that you want to reinforce, develop the specifics of your reward system, and create rules that are clear and easily understood by all employees. Make sure that targets are attainable and that all

ASK BOB AND PETER: I have found that working in a strictly commission environment causes a lot of friction. When the chips are down and a salesperson has to weigh between being slightly dishonest with a customer or coworker to make a sale and making ends meet, often the customer or coworker loses out. I have often felt that commission sales result in the staff working for the good of themselves rather than the good of the company. How can commission sales function in an organization when the very nature of this pay method promotes behavior such as being dishonest with customers, weaseling away customers from coworkers, and doing virtually anything to make a sale? Commission salespeople, by the very nature of their pay structure, are often driven to infighting. How can more positive motivation methods be implemented in this environment?

If you reward your employees—commission or otherwise—for "being dishonest with customers, weaseling away customers from coworkers," and so forth, then that's what your employees will do. To change your employees' behavior, first decide what behavior you want your employees to exhibit. Then take a very close look at your system of rewards and recognition, and make sure that it reinforces the employee behavior you want. For example, if you want your commission salespeople to cooperate with one another, then give them an incentive to do so—perhaps a cash reward for an "assist," like an assist in basketball or hockey where a player sets up a teammate to make the score. Or, have part of the honor of being top salespeople be an expectation that they share with the entire group their strategies for closing their sales. Find out from your employees what rewards motivate them the most, and use that information to reinforce the behavior you want them to exhibit.

employees have a chance to obtain rewards. For example, your clerks also should have a shot at the rewards, not just salespeople or assemblers.

- *Obtain commitment and support.* Communicate your new rewards program to your employees. Many organizations publicize their programs in group meetings. Present the programs as positive and fun activities that benefit both the employees and the company. To get the best results, plan and implement your rewards program with your employees' direct involvement.
- *Monitor effectiveness.* Is your rewards system getting the results that you want? If not, take another look at the behaviors you want to reinforce, and make sure that your rewards are closely linked. Even the most successful rewards programs tend to lose their effectiveness over time as employees begin to take them for granted. Keep your program fresh by discontinuing rewards that have lost their luster and bringing in new ones from time to time.

TEN GREAT WAYS TO MOTIVATE EMPLOYEES

Use the following checklist of effective techniques to keep your employees involved and motivated on an ongoing basis.

1. Personally thank employees for doing a good job—one on one, in writing, or both. Do it timely, often, and sincerely.
2. Take the time to meet with and listen to employees—as much as they need or want.
3. Provide employees with specific and frequent feedback about their performance. Support them in improving performance.
4. Recognize, reward, and promote high performers; deal with low and marginal performers so that they improve or leave.

THE REAL WORLD

It's relatively easy to have happy employees: Give them what they want, when they want it. Far more difficult, however, is to have employees be excited about the job and objectives you most need them to do. The process of getting someone "up" for that challenge—and keeping them up—is a moving target and never-ending challenge for any manager. Today, this is best done by starting with what is important to your employees and then achieving what is important to the organization within that context. In other words, you need to have your employees truly feel you are on their side, willing to do whatever is necessary to help them to succeed. If someone has a good boss, that is, a person who values and respects his or her employees on a consistent basis day in and day out, that person tends to feel he or she has a good job—the two go hand in hand. This requires a realization that the strength of any relationship can be measured by the last interaction. If you truly trust and respect someone else, it shows in every interaction.

5. Provide information on how the company makes and loses money, upcoming products, and services and strategies for competing. Explain the employee's role in the overall plan.

6. Involve employees in decisions, especially those decisions that affect them. Involvement equals commitment.

7. Give employees a chance to grow and develop new skills; encourage them to be their best. Show them how you can help them meet their goals while achieving the organization's goals. Create a partnership with each employee.

8. Provide employees with a sense of ownership in their work and their work environment. This ownership can be symbolic (e.g., business cards for all employees, whether they need them to do their jobs or not).

9. Strive to create a work environment that is open, trusting, and fun. Encourage new ideas, suggestions, and initiative. Learn from, rather than punish for, mistakes.

10. Celebrate successes—of the company, of the department, and of individuals. Take time for team- and morale-building meetings and activities. Be creative and fresh.

─────────── **POP QUIZ!** ───────────

What motivates people motivates them, and it changes from person to person and for any one person over time. This is what makes employee motivation so challenging: It's a moving target. Answer the following questions based on the research and information we shared in this chapter:

1. Think of the best manager you ever had. What did that person do to best motivate you in your job?

2. Although money is important to people, what other things are often considered even more important by today's employees?

3. What's the greatest management principle in the world and an example of how it works? Does this principle apply in any relationship? Explain.

4. What's the best way to determine what is most important to your employees?

5. Recognition is all around us every day, just waiting for us to tap into it. Name three examples of recognition that don't require any money.

CHAPTER 5

Coaching and Development

IT'S A NEW WORLD OUT THERE . . .

Coaching and . . .

How to create a high-performance organization.

What coaches do.

Coaching explained.

Day-to-day coaching.

The tools you'll need.

HIGH-PERFORMANCE COACHING

Over the past decade or two, there has been a major change in the way that managers do their jobs. While, in the past, managers were supposed to closely direct their employees' efforts, today's best managers are *coaches*—that is, they support and encourage the efforts of their employees. Managers who act as coaches—and not just as bosses—can help employees achieve outstanding results as their organizations perform better than ever.

But beyond supporting and encouraging the efforts of employees, coaching plays a critical part of the learning process for employees who are developing their skills, knowledge, and self-confidence. Employees will never learn to be self-sufficient when you're always telling them what to do. In fact, they usually don't learn at all, making them more reliant on you going forward, rather than less reliant.
As the old saying goes:

- Tell me . . . I forget.
- Show me . . . I remember.
- Involve me . . . I learn.

It's difficult for employees to learn effectively when you assign new tasks with no instruction or support whatsoever. Most employees will eventually figure out what to do (assuming they don't get bored first or tired of trying), but they're going to waste a lot of time feeling their way around.

Fortunately, there is a place between the two extremes of being told what to do and being given no support whatsoever. This is the place where employees are coached to learn how to work effectively, how to set and achieve goals, and how to make their own decisions. By supporting and coaching their employees, managers don't just create happier employees, they unlock the creativity and energy within their employees that make them much more effective in their jobs—improving their organizations' bottom lines in the process.

WHAT COACHES DO

So, what exactly is a coach? A coach is someone who acts as a colleague, counselor, and cheerleader to his or her employees. By encouraging their employees and supporting them when they need it, coaches help employees reach their full potential.

While we're not big fans of the metaphor of business manager as sports coach, there are definitely parallels. A football coach doesn't go out on the field and run plays or throw the football or tackle members of the opposing team. He is not allowed to actually play the game— he can only teach his players ways to improve their skills and performance, and then support and encourage them on game day.

Similarly, smart managers don't do their employees' jobs for them (as tempting as it may be). Instead, they give their employees the tools they need to do their jobs (training, money, resources), the authority they need to get their jobs done, and the support and encouragement they need to persevere through difficult circumstances. Then they stand back and get out of the way.

There are a number of things that coaches do. The following list summarizes the most important:

- *Coaches set goals.* Every organization makes plans and sets goals to achieve them. One key job of coaches is to work with their employees to set goals and deadlines for completion. The best coaches don't create these goals in a vacuum; they involve employees in defining their goals and setting deadlines for completion. They then get out of the way and allow their employees to determine exactly how to accomplish the goals.

- *Coaches support and encourage.* No one ever said that business was easy, in fact, it can sometimes be downright difficult. As a result, it's easy for employees—regardless of their level of experience or expertise—to become discouraged. Coaches keep close tabs on their employees to monitor their emotional states of mind. When employees need a boost, these managers are there to help provide it.

- *Coaches emphasize team success over individual success.* The best managers know that it's important to put the emphasis on team and team performance, not on the one or two standouts who invariably are a part of every team. Winning takes the combined efforts of all team members and singling out one or two stars only serves to demotivate the rest of the team.

- *Coaches can quickly assess the talents and shortfalls of team members.* No employee is strong in every area; some are proficient at certain tasks while others are proficient at a completely different set. It's up to coaches to determine their team members' strengths and weaknesses and then tailor their approach to each. If, for example, an employee is great at customer relations, but needs help with filling out sales reports, the manager can concentrate on providing support for the employee's development of better reporting skills.

- *Coaches teach.* Coaches are often more experienced at performing certain tasks than the employees they manage, and one of their key functions is to transfer this knowledge to employees so that they can perform at a high level of expertise. Smart coaches take the time to teach employees the skills they need to succeed in their organizations in a nonthreatening and inclusive way.

- *Coaches inspire their team members.* Employees respond positively to sincere encouragement from managers. Coaches make a point of supporting and inspiring their team members, helping them to consistently bring their best efforts to their jobs. Experienced coaches know that teams of inspired individuals can move mountains when it comes to achieving their organization's goals, and they help them do just that.

- *Coaches create environments that allow individuals to be successful.* A company's culture has to support and reward employees' giving their best efforts, otherwise, they won't bother. Managers are in the perfect position to create environments that encourage employees to make their own decisions and to make (honest) mistakes without fear of punishment. Smart coaches know that this is the way that they will get the best performance from their employees, while keeping employee morale and spirits high.

- *Coaches provide feedback.* While it's important for managers to keep track of how employees are performing, it's just as important for managers to communicate this information to their employees on a timely, candid, and complete basis. With this information in hand, employees can understand in which areas they need to improve. They can then request manager support (in the form of training or other resources) in helping them improve their efforts.

COACHING IN THREE EASY STEPS

As we point out earlier in this chapter, one of the key things that coaches do is to teach their employees. One of our favorite teaching models is what we call the *show-and-tell* method. Show-and-tell coaching consists of three distinct steps:

Step 1: You do; you say. In this first step, the coach meets with her employee and explains a procedure or task in general terms while performing it. So, for example, the coach explains how to fill out an online purchase request while actually sitting at the computer, bringing up the proper screens, and filling in a sample request.

> **? ASK BOB AND PETER:** I am the Cyber Cafe owner in Malaysia. I don't know why my staff members here are so lazy, and the motivation or encouragement that I am giving them is really not effective. What can I do to encourage my employees to be better workers?
>
> The big question is: Why are your employees unmotivated? To answer this question, you'll need to look very closely at your organization and at yourself. First, you'll need to find out if there are demotivators in the workplace. Do your employees have the tools they need to do their jobs well? Are they paid a fair wage? Are they trusted and invited to share their ideas with you? If not, you have a problem. Identify demotivators and neutralize them. Next, create a system of rewards and recognition that will encourage your employees to be motivated and excited about their work. To do this most effectively, you'll need to ask your employees what motivates them, and then find ways to make these things happen. Some employees are motivated when the boss tells them they did a good job. Others are motivated by being given more responsibility, authority, or learning opportunities. Still others are motivated by material things such as cash, gifts, or awards.

Step 2: They do; you say. The next step is for the coach to have the employee do the same procedure as the coach explains each step.

Step 3: They do; they say. Finally, as the coach observes, the employees perform the task again as they explain to the coach what they are doing.

And here's a tip from one coach to another: It also never hurts to have employees create a "cheat sheet" of the new steps they learned. This job aid is invaluable at helping new behaviors become habit for your employees.

LEVERAGING TURNING POINTS

The vast majority of a manager's job consists of the daily shaping of talents and chipping away at problems to achieve desired objectives, not in the huge win or the big splash that blows the competition out of the water. Sure, most managers get to experience the occasional big success that makes the day-to-day routine worth enduring, but it's often the little things that count when it comes to business.

That's why the best coaches are always keeping an eye out for *turning points*—the daily opportunities to succeed that are available to any employee who takes the time to look for and then act on them.

The big wins don't often happen overnight or out of the blue; they are instead a direct result of building a foundation of numerous smaller wins along the way. Meeting a difficult customer's needs, finding a way to shave a few more dollars off the unit cost of a best-selling product, inspiring an employee to redouble his efforts in the face of adversity—all are turning points, and each one builds to larger successes. Good coaches know that by focusing on the right activities, the right results aren't far behind.

A COACH A DAY

Coaching is a daily event, not just something to be brought out and dusted off for special occasions. The best coaches spend time with employees to help them succeed and they complement and supplement the abilities and experience of their employees by bringing their own abilities and experience to the table. Coaches reward their employees when they achieve their goals, and they help their employees learn important lessons when they make mistakes—and every employee no matter how good makes mistakes.

Let's walk through an example of how to deal with an employee who needs coaching. Use the following guidelines when coaching an employee:

ASK BOB AND PETER: How can you motivate a person to be a team player after a long period of time as a loner? This person is very confrontational, has strong dislike/distrust of management, and is a union employee.

Your question brings up a couple of points. Any employee who distrusts management probably has a reason (or two or three or more) for feeling that way. In a case like this, it's likely that managers in his or her past have failed to uphold promises or commitments made to the employee—and probably on more than one occasion. The first thing you have to do is to build a bridge of trust between the employee and yourself. Depending on the employee, this can potentially take a very long time. However, if you keep your promises and if you are fair in your dealings with all of your employees, you can establish trust with even the most negative worker. Second, reward the behavior you want to see more of. Put your employee in situations where he or she has to work in a team setting. Assign him or her to a self-managing team, to an employee committee, or to work on a community project. Then reinforce any positive team behavior that he or she exhibits. This doesn't have to be with money—a simple word of thanks or a written note making a big deal about an employee's accomplishment can be very effective. Above all, be patient. It's probably taken your employee a long time to get to the place where you find him or her now. It will probably take a long time to get this employee to the place you envision. But get moving in that direction, one step at a time.

- *Meet with your employee.* Before you can coach, you've first got to meet with your employee. Make an appointment with your employee as soon as you can after the issue or problem is apparent. Be sure to choose a location that is quiet and free of distractions— your office will probably be the ideal place—and hold your phone calls or forward your phone to voice mail.

THE REAL WORLD

All development is self-development, yet at the same time, having someone who can help coach us allows us to achieve more in our work and lives along the way. Who's one of the greatest golfers alive today? If you said Tiger Woods, know that he has a coach to help him keep at his best and improve. Every manager serves as a coach for his or her employees, helping them to become the best they can be in their jobs. It's a responsibility that should be taken seriously, with planned feedback sessions and specific plans for improvement. It's also a responsibility that can be chipped away at every day at work. Any given assignment, for example, can also be a learning opportunity for an employee to stretch and grow, learning new skills that can be applied in other ways for years to come. And a steady stream of feedback can make it easier for employees to fine-tune their performance.

- *Listen!* Too many people love to talk, but too few love to listen. When you listen to an employee, she will be extremely motivated because you're demonstrating to her that she is important enough for you to take time out of your busy schedule to focus on her. Ask your employee to bring you up to date with the situation, her concerns, and any possible approaches or solutions considered. Let her do the talking while you do the listening.
- *Reinforce the positive.* Before you point out areas that need improvement, it's important to first point out the things that your employee did right in the particular situation. Be sure to let your employee know when she is on the right track. And do it now, don't wait until later!

- *Highlight areas for improvement.* As we mentioned earlier, every employee has areas in which performance can be improved. Explore with your employee the assistance that you can provide, whether your employee needs more budgetary resources, additional training, or whatever is necessary. Be sure your employee knows that you are confident in her ability to do a great job.
- *Follow through.* Once you make a promise to support your employee, then be sure to follow up on your side of the bargain. There's little more demotivating than a manager who promises one thing, then does something else.

And don't forget to be patient. Not everyone is the same, and some people will make progress faster than others. It's your job to assess the differences in abilities among your employees, and then to use that knowledge to tailor your approach appropriately.

TOOLS OF THE TRADE

As a coach, you'll undertake a wide range of activities, tailored to the specific needs of your individual employees. In some cases, this may mean nothing more than an occasional, informal progress check while making the rounds of the office. In other, more extreme cases, this may mean scheduling frequent, formal meetings with the employee to provide intensive coaching on an ongoing basis.

Every coach has his or her unique approach to coaching; here are some of the best:

- *Make time for team members.* How can you expect your employees to make time for your organization and your customers if you don't make time to for your employees? While you cannot be at their unlimited disposal every waking minute of every day, they shouldn't have to make an appointment six months in advance for a five-minute discussion. Remember that your employees are your number one priority and act accordingly.

- *Provide context and vision.* Instead of simply telling employees what to do, the best coaches explain why. Coaches provide their employees with perspective and they help them see how their work fits into the big picture. Rather than creating long lists of dos and don'ts, effective coaches demonstrate how the organization works and then lets employees choose their own path within it.

- *Transfer knowledge and perspective.* Most coaches have more experience and expertise than the people they are coaching—at least in the areas that are being coached. It's the coach's job and duty to spread that experience and expertise broadly around the organization and not to hoard it for some distant day.

- *Be a sounding board.* Because coaches have often been through the same problems or responded to the same opportunities as their employees are experiencing, they make great sounding boards. Employees can run their ideas by a coach to get an opinion before they implement them—possibly averting a disastrous outcome. Effective coaches help their employees work through issues and come up with the best solutions themselves.

- *Obtain needed resources.* Employees may simply need additional resources to make the jump from marginal to outstanding performance. It's a coach's job to be attentive to these needs and to do whatever he or she can to help provide the needed resources, whether time, money, staff, equipment, or other assets.

- *Offer a helping hand.* Learning a new job or procedure can be an overwhelming experience for an employee. Coaches help workers make it over the hump by reassigning current duties to other employees, authorizing overtime, or taking other measures to allow overwhelmed employees to come up for air and catch their breath.

———————————————— **POP QUIZ!** ————————————

Coaching is one of the most fundamental—and elusive—skills of managing. Check your knowledge of what it takes to be a good coach:

1. A good coach is demanding, but fair. How can you best balance these two dimensions?
2. What are the three steps of foolproof coaching?
3. As a coach, you need great patience. How is your patience in working with and managing others? How could you improve?
4. Coaching is a developmental process that can best be done by looking for what type of opportunities for learning?
5. What are the steps of an effective coaching session?

CHAPTER 6

Mentoring Employees

IT'S A NEW WORLD OUT THERE . . .

Developing and mentoring employees and . . .

Helping them improve their performance.

The purpose of developing and mentoring employees.

Creating career development plans.

The best career development strategies.

Becoming a mentor yourself.

BUILDING BETTER EMPLOYEES

Why is it that so many employees are hired with the best of intentions and then—a few days or weeks after they arrive—they are promptly forgotten? It's easy to take the orientation and training needs of employees—both new and veteran—for granted. Managers are busy people and so long as there's no crisis, then there are more important things to attend to. Right?

Wrong.

In every organization, employees have so much to figure out: formal and informal chains of command, the ins and outs of office politics, the right and wrong ways to get the support and resources you need to get your job done, which people are "in"—and which are "out." And this is just the beginning; employees also have to learn new skills and techniques to improve the way they do their jobs. All of this requires training, and it requires the attention of the managers who are responsible for ensuring their employees have the opportunity to develop their talents.

But here's the rub: Employee development doesn't just happen. For employees to learn new skills and develop their expertise and knowledge, both managers and employees must make a concerted effort to ensure employment development stays at or near the top of everyone's list of priorities. Believe us—the results will be well worth the effort.

WHY DEVELOP YOUR EMPLOYEES?

So, why bother developing your employees? One key reason is that your employees will learn a variety of new skills that will make them better and more effective in their jobs. Not only will they do a better job for their organizations, they will do a better job for their customers—earning their long-term business and loyalty in the process. Another key reason for developing your employees is that they will transfer the skills they learn to other employees in your organization—multiplying the impact of your development efforts many times over. Finally, when you spend time developing your employees, you are sending a message loud and clear: Your employees are important to you and worth your time and attention. And employees who feel that you think they are important are employees who *will* become important, bringing with them a high level of loyalty and commitment.

But, before we get into the details of what employee training and development is all about, let's first establish exactly what it is that we're talking about.

Training usually refers to teaching workers the short-term skills that they need to know right now to do their jobs. *Development* usually refers to teaching employees the kinds of long-term skills that they'll need as they progress in their careers. In many organizations, employee development is instead known as *career development*.

We'll ask the question again: Why bother developing your employees? As it turns out, there are plenty of good reasons, including:

- *You may be taking your employees' knowledge for granted.* Just because your employees aren't having obvious problems doing their jobs, that doesn't necessarily mean that they are doing their *best* jobs, or that there isn't room for improvement. You may have looked at hundreds of resumes to fill a particular position, and interviewed a boatload of people before you found the right person for the job. And while you might assume that this individual knows everything there is to know about the job to be done, there's a good chance that he doesn't. Every organization has its own unique approach to doing business, and even the most knowledgeable employee can learn something new. That's where employee development comes in.

- *Employees who work smarter are better employees.* Wouldn't it be great if all of your employees worked at 100 percent of their potential, at least most of the time? While no employee can possibly be 100-percent effective every moment of every working day (even robots need the occasional maintenance break), employees who are better trained and more knowledgeable about their jobs have the potential to do a much better job than employees who aren't. Employees who have achieved their development goals simply work smarter. Not only will your organization reap the benefits in greater employee efficiency and effectiveness (well worth the price of admission), but also you'll sleep better at night—something any manager in any business can appreciate.

- *Someone has to be prepared to step into your shoes.* Although it may be hard to imagine right now, someday you may decide to retire, or you may be promoted and moved up the career ladder. Who is going to take your place when you're gone? Developing employees is all about providing them with the skills they need to be able to step into your shoes in your absence. And, while you might not be retiring or getting promoted anytime soon, you might like to take a week or two off. Have you ever envied fellow managers who don't have to call their offices when they are on vacation? They are able to unplug from their offices because they make a point of developing their employees so they are able to take over when the manager is gone. Guess what? You can, too.

- *Your employee wins, and so does your organization.* Your employees win when you provide them with higher-level skills and new ways of viewing the world. And, at the same time, your organization wins because employees become more motivated and their work skills improve. The impact of every dollar spent on employee development is therefore magnified while employees are prepared to fill the roles in which your organization will need them to move in the future.

- *Your employees are worth your time and money.* It costs a lot of money to recruit and hire new employees, and it costs a lot to train them. Employees are one of any organization's greatest investments, and it's in your interest as a manager to ensure that these investments are protected and allowed to flourish. By backing up with action your words of support for employees, you show them that you really mean what you say—leading to employees who are more engaged in their jobs and who will better serve your customers.

CAREER DEVELOPMENT PLANS

Sometimes you can get where you want to go in business—if you're lucky. But, more often, it takes a plan, and effective career development requires well thought out and executed plans. Make no mistake about it: Career development plans take time to develop and they take time to monitor, track, and adjust as needed. But the investment of time required will pay off many times over in employees who perform better and who are happier in their jobs.

The best career development plans contain at minimum the following five key elements:

1. *Specific learning goals:* By identifying specific *learning goals* with your employees—classes they should take, skills they should learn, expertise they should develop—you provide them with a clearly marked path to travel as they proceed through their careers. The learning goals for a contract negotiator might, for example, include coursework in contract law, negotiation techniques workshops, and a progression of assignments from relatively simple low-dollar negotiations to very complex, high-dollar deals.
2. *Resources required to achieve the designated learning goals:* It's not enough to create learning goals; managers also have to designate the organizational resources that will be devoted to making the

goals happen. Such resources might include assignment to specific teams or job shadowing, formal training (conducted by outsiders, by internal trainers, or perhaps online), and of course the money required to pay for all this.

3. *Employee responsibilities and resources:* Career development is a joint responsibility of an employee and his or her manager. A business can and does pay for things, but so can employees (as any employee who has paid out of his own pocket to get a college degree can attest). A good career development plan should include what the employee is doing on his or her own time.

4. *Required date of completion for each learning goal:* Every good plan also needs a good schedule, so therefore each learning goal must have a corresponding date of completion. Schedules must be above all else realistic while keeping an employee's forward progress in motion. Ideally, schedules will allow employees the flexibility to get their daily tasks done while keeping a step ahead of the changes in the business environment that necessitate the employees' development in the first place.

5. *Standards for measuring the accomplishment of learning goals:* Of course, employees and their managers must have some way of knowing when (and if) a learning goal has been completed. Standards might be unambiguous (a course has been completed) or it might be more subjective (the employee has some measure of expertise in a particular area of learning). Whatever the situation, managers should always ensure that the selected standards are clear and attainable and that both you and your employees are in full agreement with them.

Are you by now wondering what a simple career development plan might look like? Here's an example of a basic career development plan for an interest rate analyst. Note that a career development plan doesn't have to be complicated and it doesn't have to be as big as the book that you're holding in your hands. When it comes to employee plans of any sort, simpler (and more concise) is usually better:

PETER SORKIN'S CAREER DEVELOPMENT PLAN

SKILL GOAL

- Become proficient in interest rate analysis.

LEARNING GOAL

- Learn the basics of employee supervision.

PLAN

- Shadow supervisor in daily work for half days, starting immediately.
- Attend quarterly supervisors' update seminar on the first Wednesday of January, April, July, and October (no cost: in-house).
- Complete "Basics of Interest Rate Analysis" class no later than the first quarter of fiscal year XX ($550 plus travel costs).
- Successfully complete "Intermediate Interest Rate Analysis" class no later than the second quarter of fiscal year XX ($750 plus travel costs).
- Continue self-funded accounting certificate program at local community college.

This career development plan contains each of the five necessary elements as described earlier. Remember: Career development plans don't have to be complicated to be effective. The exact format of the plan is not important; what's important is that you create career development plans for your employees.

HELPING TO DEVELOP EMPLOYEES

The role of the manager in developing employees is to help employees figure out exactly what they want to go, and then to provide the support and organizational resources for employees to get there. But employee development is a two-way street, and managers cannot take on this task in a vacuum. Employees must also participate by identifying the areas where development will help to make them better and more productive workers in the future and relaying this information to their managers. Once needs are identified, plans developed, and resources identified, managers and employees can work together to turn them into reality.

In the following steps, we'll explore the best way for managers to approach the development process with their employees.

Step 1: Meet with your employees about their careers. What's the best way to determine the path your employees want to take in their careers? Ask them! You might, for example, think that your top software engineer has her sights set on your organization's chief technology officer position, when she would actually much rather keep coding software. Once you determine where in the organization your employee wants her career to go, then you'll have a baseline from which to work.

Step 2: Discuss your employees' strengths and weaknesses. Every employee has certain areas of strengths, and other areas of weakness. A decision will have to be made: Do you further develop an employee's strengths (making him the best die cutter in the business), or do you try to shore up weaknesses (turning a lone wolf, for example, into a team player)? Or do you do both? Be frank with your employee about both his strengths and weaknesses, and then decide where you will direct your focus and resources. Our own feeling is that it's more important to develop your employees' strengths (further increasing their value to the organization, along with their self-esteem) than to improve their weaknesses (which may raise these areas only to the barely adequate at best).

Step 3: Assess where your employees are now. A career plan is like a story arc—there is a beginning, an end, and a lot of events in between. To better understand where your employee should go, you've got to first determine where she is now. By assessing the current state of her skills and talents, you'll end up with an overall road map to guide your development efforts.

Step 4: Create career development plans. A career development plan formalizes the agreements that you make to provide formal support (tuition, time off, travel expenses, and so on) to your employee in developing his or her career. Effective career development plans contain milestones for the achievement of learning goals and descriptions of any other resources and support needed to meet the goals that you agree to.

Step 5: Follow through on your agreements, and make sure that your employees follow through on theirs. Once you agree on specific career development plans with your employees, be sure that you uphold your end of the bargain, and that your employees uphold their end as well. Be sure to check your employees' progress regularly—once every quarter would not be too often—and if they miss schedules because of other priorities, reassign their work as necessary to ensure that they have the time they need to focus on their career development plans.

Career development is something that tends to get put off because of other priorities. And, even when it is conducted on a regular basis, the frequency of discussions is often few and far in between. Many managers, for example, conduct career discussions only when they conduct annual employee performance appraisals. While this is certainly better than never having career development discussions at all, this really isn't often enough—especially as most businesses find themselves in a state of constant whitewater change, where markets and technology are anything but stable and predictable.

Ask Bob and Peter: I am an office manager of a doctor's office, and we recently added a new doctor. This new doctor has chosen one staff member to be his "pet." He has asked that we lighten her load, pitch in to help her, and so on. When I instructed her in writing to complete a project previously assigned, he told her she did not have to do it because my request that she explain why she had again failed to do something was too harsh. Please offer your suggestions.

We all have favorites in our personal and business lives—people with whom we prefer to spend our time. However, when a business owner or manager gives preferential treatment to certain employees over others for reasons that aren't based on their performance, there is a serious problem—one that must be addressed immediately. As office manager, it's your job to supervise the administrative staff. The new doctor is not only confusing the lines of authority within the office but also undermining your ability to get your job done. Our advice is to first sit down with the new doctor for a little heart-to-heart discussion. Explain that it's not fair to the rest of your staff when he plays favorites and that his actions are creating confusion about who is really supposed to be in charge (you!). If he doesn't take your message to heart, approach the other doctors in your office and ask for their help. They may not be aware that there is a problem, and once they are, they should realize that it's in their best interest to fix it. Good luck!

The Top 10 Ways to Develop Employees

1. Provide employees with opportunities to learn and grow.
2. Be a mentor to an employee.
3. Let an employee fill in for you in staff meetings.
4. Assign your employee to a team.
5. Allow employees to pursue and develop their ideas.

6. Provide employees with a choice of assignments.
7. Send your employee to a seminar on a new topic.
8. Take an employee along with you when you call on customers.
9. Introduce your employee to top managers in your organization, and arrange to have him or her perform special assignments for them.
10. Allow an employee to shadow you during your workday.

HOW TO BE A MENTOR

Most business leaders are familiar with the power of mentoring, a relationship in which a person with greater experience and wisdom guides another to a higher level of personal and professional excellence. In fact, the vast majority of business executives have experienced successful mentoring relationships first hand. In a recent survey of Fortune 1000 executives sponsored by Robert Half International, 94 percent of respondents stated that having a mentor is important for individuals early in their careers and 75 percent reported that they currently have a mentor or have had one in the past.

While formal mentoring programs in business are a relatively recent phenomenon, James Cash Penney in 1901 was an early proponent of formal mentoring as a way of developing managers to build new J.C. Penney stores. The history of mentoring is very long and very rich. The term *mentor* comes from the ancient Greek myth of Odysseus. According to legend, when King Odysseus prepared to leave home on a ten-year journey to fight in the Trojan War, he asked his loyal friend Mentor to protect, guide, and teach his young and inexperienced son Telemachus. Mentor—actually, the goddess Athena in disguise—gladly did Odysseus's bidding, guiding Telemachus's development, becoming his trusted advisor, and teaching him important lessons about life.

In business today, mentoring most typically refers to the pairing up of an older, more experienced employee—often a manager—with a younger, less experienced employee. Researchers point to numerous

---

THE REAL WORLD

We all need heroes and role models in our lives, and this is all the more true when it comes to our careers. Most people will spend more time planning their next vacation than they will ever give to planning their career. Having a mentor helps to give you a perspective—and needed feedback—on your job, career, and profession. Chances are, however, getting a mentor will not happen by accident! You need to think about whom you can best learn from and approach him or her about the opportunity. Perhaps initially, meet the potential mentor for lunch and ask for advice about an issue in your job. If the individual is helpful and supportive, you can expand the types of things that you ask for advice about, and, at some point, ask if he or she would be interested in being an ongoing advisor for you. Most people are honored to be asked to be an ongoing advisor for someone's career.

---

benefits of mentoring relationships for both mentor and protégé, and to the organizations for which they work. In one study, executives who had a mentor earned higher incomes at an earlier age than executives who did not have a mentor. In another study, protégés reported a greater commitment toward their organizations, higher job satisfaction, better socialization, a greater sense of career progress, and higher salaries and promotions as a result of their mentoring experiences.

There are two main types of mentoring programs in common use today: formal and informal. Formal programs create prescribed processes for identifying prospective mentors and protégés and then pairing them up. Informal programs have no prescribed pairing processes, instead relying on mentors and protégés to self select. While both kinds of mentoring programs are commonly used, it is increasingly clear from both the research and the practical application of mentoring programs in a wide variety of organizational settings that formal mentoring programs are more successful, producing more and better quality mentor-protégé relationships.

Mentors benefit organizations—and the employees within them—in a variety of different ways, including:

- *Explaining how the organization really works.* Experienced employees know how their organizations *really* work—both in their formal and in their informal procedures, processes, and cultures. A mentor will have a very good understanding of what the company's formal pronouncements really mean, and he or she can convey that knowledge to other, less experienced, employees without their having to figure it out the hard way.

- *Teaching by example.* Effective mentors know the best ways to get things done in organizations, and they can teach other employees these same lessons. There's no reason every employee should have to figure out how to get things done by themselves when there are experienced employees around who can show them the ropes.

- *Providing growth experiences.* Mentors are highly qualified to guide employees to activities above and beyond their formal career development plans that will be helpful to their career growth and progress. So, while an employee's career development plan might be silent in the area of learning how to speak Spanish, a mentor might understand that making the suggestion that an employee attend community college Spanish classes would be of great benefit to him due to changing customer demographics.

- *Providing career guidance and discussion.* Above all, mentors make great sounding boards, and they are usually a safe place for employees to be frank and honest with assessments of their own progress and how they fit within their organizations. The informal discussions that mentors and employees engage in are extremely valuable to the employees, and—ultimately—to the companies for which they work.

—————————————— POP QUIZ! ——————————————

A great manager will almost always be skilled at developing and mentoring employees. Reflect on the contents of this chapter in answering these questions:

1. What are benefits to developing your employees?
2. How can you better help your employees to learn and grow?
3. Name three specific actions you can use to give an employee increased responsibility.
4. Have you ever had a mentor in your work life or career? If so, what did you most value and learn from that person?
5. What are ways you can help mentor other employees in your organization?

PART

Execution: Getting the Job Done

CHAPTER 7

Setting Goals

IT'S A NEW WORLD OUT THERE . . .

Setting Goals and . . .

The purpose of goals.

SMART goals made easy.

Communicating goals and vision.

Maintaining focus on your goals.

Making goals happen.

GOALS MAKE THINGS HAPPEN

"All performance starts with clear goals" is one of the most time-tested principles of management. What is the primary duty of management? Setting goals is likely to be near the top of the list. If setting goals appears near the bottom of the list, you know there's a problem. In most companies, top management sets the overall purpose—the vision—of the organization. Middle managers then have the job of developing goals and plans for achieving the vision set by top management. Managers and employees work together to set goals and develop schedules for attaining them.

Managers are immersed in goals—not only for themselves but also for their employees, your department, and your organization. This flood of goals can overwhelm managers as they gallantly try to balance their relative importance. Goals help provide your employees with direction and purpose; they help them see where they're going and how they can get there. And the *way* you go about setting goals can impact how motivating (or demotivating) they are to your employees.

If you want to get somewhere meaningful in your business, you and your employees first have to know where to go. And once you've decided where to go, the next step is to make plans on how to get there.

Let's say you have a vision of starting up a new technology incubator in Toronto, Ontario. If you want to achieve this vision, you have three basic approaches:

1. An unplanned, non-goal-oriented approach.
2. A planned, goal-oriented approach.
3. A hope and a prayer.

Which of these three approaches is the most likely to help you achieve your goal (or at least move in the right direction)? A planned, goal-oriented approach is the one that will have the best chance of working.

If you want to accomplish something significant, here are a number of key reasons why you should set goals:

- *Goals provide direction.* If you are planning to start up a new technology incubator in Toronto, there are plenty of different ways to achieve this particular result. The first step, however, is to set a definite vision—a target to aim for and to guide the efforts of you and your organization. Once you have a definite vision, you can translate it into goals that will help you bring your vision to reality.
- *Goals tell you how far you've traveled.* When your goals have dates assigned for their accomplishment, they become milestones along the road to bringing your vision to life. By noting what milestones have been achieved, you know exactly how many remain to reach your vision.
- *Goals help to make your overall vision attainable.* While you might be able to achieve your vision in one big step if you devoted enough resources to the task, it's often smarter (and more realistic) to take many small steps to get there. If your vision is to open a new technology incubator in Toronto, you can't expect to proclaim your vision on Wednesday and walk into a fully staffed and functioning office on Thursday. There are lots of smaller goals—from obtaining office space, to recruiting staff, and much more—to accomplish on the road to achieving your vision. By dividing your efforts into smaller pieces, goals enable you to achieve your overall vision.
- *Goals give people something to strive for.* When challenged to reach goals beyond their normal level of performance, employees are more highly motivated than when goals are too easy to achieve. Design goals that stretch your employees—goals that they will have to strive to accomplish.

Goals must link directly to an organization's vision to be useful. Managers create compelling visions, and they then work with employees to set and achieve the goals to reach those visions. The best goals:

- Are few in number and specific in purpose.
- Are stretch goals—not too easy, not too difficult.
- Involve people—when you involve others, you get buy-in so it becomes their goal, not just yours.

The importance of setting goals and planning is illustrated by venture capitalist and marketing communications expert Debra Jones. She tells businesspeople to remember that they have 100 balls in the air at any given time. Eighty-five of those balls are rubber; if they drop, no harm is done. Ten of those balls are rocks—they make a big noise when they're dropped, but again, no harm is done. However, five of those balls that every businessperson juggles are made of glass—drop one of those and it shatters, creating a big problem for the organization. Setting goals and developing plans help you figure out which of the balls you're juggling are ones that, if dropped, your organization will recover and ones that, if dropped, may put your organization in peril. Do you know what kind of balls *you're* juggling?

SMART GOALS

There are all kinds of goals; some are short term and specific while others are long term and indefinite. And while some goals can be easily understood by most any employee, others can be complex and difficult to figure out. Still others can be easily accomplished while others are virtually impossible to attain.

This is all well and good, but the whole point of setting goals is to achieve them. Goals should consistently be understandable, realistic, and attainable. You're wasting your time (and your employees' time) by going to the trouble of calling meetings, involving employees, and burning precious time, only to end up with goals that cannot be achieved.

The best goals are *SMART* goals—*specific, measurable, attainable, relevant, and time-bound* (see pages 115–116).

THE BIG PICTURE

DICK DeVOS

Former President and Co-CEO, Amway Corporation

Question: How does a large business like Amway stay nimble in fast-changing markets?

Answer: What we're trying to create here is an atmosphere of nimbleness or an attitude that we're prepared to go where we need to go. Historically at this company, there's been a lot of inertia, and that inertia always works in our way. We had 40 years of doing a lot of things very much the same way, so we've been straight lining for quite a while. And while we've made minor adjustments in the course of things, it's been essentially the same basic business concept for all these years. But, because of the introduction of technology and a real fundamental change in the competitive environment, we have to look at our business in a new way and acknowledge as well that we have to take an entirely different attitude. Instead of trying to optimize in a direction because we know which direction we're going and we can optimize it, we have to recreate the mentality around here of a willingness to change, or as we've expressed it around here, we've got to learn how to do "new" better. And how to do "new" well. That's been a catch phrase we've used; doing new things is a skill that we have to acquire. And a lot of that is an attitude of getting rid of fear, fear of change, getting rid of resistance to change, viewing change as opportunity as opposed to risk or challenge, and then at the personal level, people understanding that change poses opportunity for them in their day-to-day work and their jobs; it doesn't inherently pose a risk to their security.

Question: When you're talking about three million people out there selling your products, how do you communicate that sense of immediacy to them?

Answer: Although we have a large organization, a lot of them are very tactical, they're very much involved in the here and now, and their ability or their willingness to move is already pretty good. The resistance tends to be within those who have a greater financial or time investment or longevity stack. So the individuals in our organization who have been around for a longer time or have a particular position that suits them well are now going into a period in their life where they just don't want to change much. Or they view change as having more downside than upside to them. So it's really breaking through at the more senior levels. At the more junior levels in the organization, people are pretty open. So the challenge for us is to get the blood flowing among the more entrenched group—which is a very influential group in any organization—the leadership group. In our case, that's a small enough group that it's actually something we can impact. And they in turn will set the agenda for the rest of the organization.

1. *Specific:* SMART goals are clear and unambiguous; when goals are specific, employees know exactly what's expected, when, and how much. As an extra benefit, when goals are specific, it's easy to measure employee progress toward their completion.
2. *Measurable:* SMART goals can be measured. When goals can't be measured, it's impossible to tell whether employees are making progress toward their successful completion. Not only that, but employees may be unable to sustain their motivation to complete goals when there are no milestones to indicate their progress.
3. *Attainable:* SMART goals are both realistic and attainable by the majority of employees, although it's also good to design goals so that employees have to stretch some to achieve them. Goals set too high or too low become meaningless, and employees will eventually ignore them.

4. *Relevant:* SMART goals relate to the organizations vision and mission, and they move the organization forward in some way. According to Pareto's 80/20 rule, managers should focus their effort on designing goals that address the 20 percent of workers' activities that have the greatest impact on performance while bringing the organization closer to its vision.

5. *Time-bound:* SMART goals have definite schedules with start dates, end dates, and fixed durations. When employees commit to deadlines, it helps them focus their efforts on completion of the goal on or before its due date. When goals aren't assigned deadlines or schedules for completion, they tend to be overtaken by the day-to-day crises that invariably arise in an organization and eventually are forgotten.

The SMART system of goal setting outlined above provides you with guidelines to help frame effective goals, but there are other factors to keep in mind. These factors ensure that the goals that you and your employees agree to can be easily understood and acted on by anyone in your organization:

- *Ensure that goals are related to your employees' role in the organization.* It's far easier for employees to pursue an organization's goals when those goals are made a regular part of their jobs. Goals should be assigned to employees as a part of their duties, not as something to do in their spare time, and they should directly relate to the employee's job in some way.

- *Whenever possible, use values to guide behavior.* Values such as honesty, fairness, respect, and more are important to maintaining an organization's integrity. An organization's leaders should model this behavior while rewarding employees who live it.

- *Simple goals are better goals.* Employees are much more likely to work to achieve goals when they are easy to understand. Goals should be concise, compelling, and easy to read and understand,

and no longer than a sentence. Goals that take more space than a sentence should be broken into smaller goals.

FEWER GOALS ARE BETTER GOALS

When you go to the trouble of setting goals, keep them to a manageable number that can realistically be followed up on. Having too many goals often means that nothing gets done. When it comes to goal setting, less is more.

Consider these guidelines for selecting the right goals for your organization:

- *Pick two to three goals to focus on.* People cannot realistically focus on more than a few goals at a time. Assigning employees too many goals often means that many of the goals will be ignored, resulting in haphazard results.
- *Pick the goals with the greatest relevance.* You've only got so many hours in your workday, so it makes a lot of sense to concentrate your efforts on a few goals that have the biggest payoff rather than on a boatload of goals with relatively less payoff. Constantly ask yourself, "What one or two things could have the greatest impact on our success?"
- *Focus on the goals that tie most closely to your organization's mission.* When interesting goals that are challenging, interesting, and fun to accomplish are too far removed from your organization's mission, then you're not really doing the work that the organization needs to be done. As interesting as they may be, you've got to keep your focus on the goals that are most important to the organization's long-term success.
- *Periodically revisit the goals and update them as necessary.* Markets and business environments change all the time, and so do goals. Just because a goal is relevant today, that doesn't mean that it will be

ASK BOB AND PETER: Setting goals with my employees is always difficult for me. Do you have any advice on how to best set goals?

As you know, it's one thing to set goals, and it's another thing altogether to achieve them. The best way to ensure that your goals (and your employees' goals) are achieved is to make them SMART goals: **S**pecific—goals must be clear and concise if you expect your employees to achieve them; **M**easurable—if you can't measure progress toward achieving a goal, you'll never know whether you or your employees have attained them; **A**ttainable—while it's always good to stretch a little to achieve a goal, it should never be unattainable or unrealistic; **R**elevant—employee goals should directly relate to attaining department or organizational goals; **T**ime-bound—every goal should have a defined period of time for completion. Keep these points in mind when you set goals, and you'll be on the road to success.

tomorrow. Periodically check your goals to ensure that they're still relevant to the vision you want to achieve. If they are not, meet with your employees to revise them.

Be careful not to take on too many goals at once. Not only are you in danger of being overwhelmed, but also so are your employees. It's much better to pick a few, significant goals and then focus your efforts on attaining them. Management isn't a game of huge success after huge success. Management is a daily meeting of challenges and opportunities—gradually, but inevitably, improving the organization in the process.

COMMUNICATING GOALS AND VISION

Once you have established goals for your organization, you've got to communicate them to your employees. There are many possible ways to communicate goals to your employees, but some ways are better than others (and some are worse). Whatever your approach, the goals must be communicated clearly, the receiver must understand the goals, and the goals must be followed through on by the people to whom they have been assigned.

Although communicating vision and goals to employees is equally important, your approach in doing so will be different for each. Managers usually introduce their organizations' visions publicly, and with much excitement—all the better to inspire employees with it. Here are some ways that companies commonly announce and communicate their vision:

- By way of huge employee rallies where the vision is unveiled in inspirational presentations.
- By incorporating their vision into anything possible that employees, customers, and vendors will read, including business cards, letterhead stationery, newsletters, employee name tags, and more.
- By requesting that supervisors and managers keep vision front and center in staff meetings and employee interactions.

Goals are much more personal than an organization's vision, and so the methods used to communicate them must be much more direct. Here are a few tips for communicating goals:

- First write down the goals. In the case of individual goals, conduct face-to-face meetings with employees to introduce and discuss them. To maximize their involvement and buy-in, be sure to ask for their input in the development of the goals that they will be required to achieve.
- Introduce team-related goals in a meeting specifically held to do that. As with individual goals, be sure to maximize the team's involvement and buy-in by asking for their input in the development of the goals. Get the team together to explain the role of the team and each individual in the successful completion of the goal; make

sure that every member of the team understands exactly what he or she is supposed to do.

- Request that your employees, whether individually or on teams, commit to the successful accomplishment of their goals. In addition, ask your employees to prepare and present plans and milestone schedules explaining how they will accomplish the assigned goals by the deadlines that you agreed to. Then be sure to regularly monitor employee progress to ensure that the goals are on track, and to flag problems that you can help them overcome if necessary.

MAINTAINING FOCUS ON YOUR GOALS

The goal setting process gets employees energized and excited. But the problem is that this excitement and energy can quickly evaporate the moment employees get back to their desks. It's your job as a manager to take steps to ensure that employee focus remains centered on the goals and not on other matters that are less important but momentarily more pressing.

Maintaining a focus on goals can be extremely difficult—particularly in the typical busy business environments in which most of us work. Consider the typical situations that vie for your attention during a typical day at work:

- You've got your day all planned out only to have your plans pushed aside when your boss gives you a call about some crisis that needs immediate attention.
- An employee walks in your office with a problem that needs to be solved right now.
- You get caught in a 15-minute meeting that drags on for several hours.

There are 1,001 ways you or your employees can lose the focus that you need to get your organization's goals accomplished. One of the

---

THE REAL WORLD

"All performance starts with clear goals" is a basic tenet of management. The clearer those goals can be defined, the more likely they are to be attained. The more you involve others in creating the goal, the greater is their buy-in to want to achieve it. The best goals are clear in number and specific in focus. You can't focus on everything; the longer your to-do list gets, the greater is the tendency for you to do nothing on it. By constantly prioritizing "what is most important for me to get done," you'll have the greatest chance of doing those things. If you get bogged down or off track and find yourself not focused on the most important things you should be doing, break those goals down into smaller, more achievable objectives and keep them on top of your list.

---

biggest problems with getting goals accomplished is confusing activity with results. Consider the example of the employee who gets into the office before everyone else—and who stays after everyone else goes home at night—but never seems to get anything done. While the employee is busy working, he or she is working on the wrong things. The *activity trap*, is very easy for you and your employees to fall into (and much harder to get out of).

Achieving your goals is your job. Your boss can coach and support you, but you're the one who has to concentrate on achieving your goals. This means taking charge of your work life by controlling your own schedule. Believe us: If you don't control your schedule, someone else will control your schedule for you.

Here are some tips to ensure that you and your employees stay out of the activity trap:

- *Do your first priority first.* It's tempting to work on the easy stuff first and save the tough stuff for last. And with people dropping into your office just to chat or to unload their problems on you, concentrating on your first priority is a constant challenge. If you don't do your first priority first, however, you're almost guaranteed to find yourself in the activity trap, which means that you'll find the same priorities on your list of tasks day after day, week after week, and month after month. This is not a plan for accomplishing your goals. Keep your eye on the prize by doing first things first.

- *Get organized.* To be effective in business, you've got to get organized and manage your time effectively. When you're organized, you can spend less time trying to figure out what you should be doing and more time doing what you should be doing.
- *Just say no!* When you're a manager, your employees are guaranteed to constantly try to make their problems your problems. This is bad for a couple of reasons: It distracts you from focusing on solving your own problems, and if you solve your employees' problems for them, they'll never learn the problem-solving skills that they need to progress in their careers and within the organization. Before taking on someone else's problem, ask yourself, "How does this help me achieve my goals?" Focus on your own goals, and refuse to let others make their problems your own.

MAKING GOALS HAPPEN

Whether you are a manager or employee, you have the power to make your goals happen by controlling or influencing people and events around you on a daily basis. Generally, power is a positive thing, but it can be a negative thing when abused. Manipulation, exploitation, and coercion are all examples of power gone bad, and they have no place in the modern workplace.

Use the positive power within you to your advantage by tapping into it to help achieve your organization's goals. Every employee has five primary sources of power in an organization, and he or she has specific strengths and weaknesses related to these sources. Consider your own personal strengths and weaknesses as you review the five sources of power that follow:

1. *Personal power:* This is the power that comes from within your character, and it includes your passion for greatness, the strength of your convictions, your ability to communicate and inspire, your personal charisma, and your leadership skills.

2. *Relationship power:* Your day-to-day interactions with others at work contribute to the relationship power that you wield on the job. Common sources of relationship power include close friendships with top executives, partners, or owners; people who owe you favors; and coworkers who provide you with information and insights that you would normally not get through your formal business relationships.

3. *Knowledge power:* Knowledge power is the specific expertise and knowledge that you have gained during the course of your career as well as the knowledge you acquire as a result of training or the pursuit of academic degrees such as an MBA.

4. *Task power:* Task power is the power that comes from the job or process that you perform at work. As you have undoubtedly witnessed on many occasions, people can facilitate or impede the efforts of their coworkers and others through the application of task power. For example, when you submit a claim for payment to your insurance company and months pass with no action, you are on the receiving end of task power.

5. *Position power:* Position power refers to your rank or title in the organization and is a function of the authority that you wield to command human and financial resources. As a manager, your position power is relatively high in the organization. But, remember that the best leaders seldom rely on position power to get things done today—they instead use their own charisma, knowledge, and relationships to convince others to get things done.

Be aware of the sources of your power in your life, and use your power in a positive way to help you and your employees accomplish the goals of your organization. If you're stronger in some areas than others, be sure to work on improving your weak points while leveraging the areas where your power is strong. And remember: A little power can go a long way. Try not to overdo it.

─────────────── **POP QUIZ!** ───────────────

Setting goals is an important way for managers to get things done in their organizations. Reflect for a few moments on what you have learned in this chapter; then ask yourself the following questions:

1. What process of goal setting do you follow?
2. What do you do to involve your employees in the goal-setting process?
3. How do you keep track of employee progress toward achievement of their goals?
4. In what ways do you support your employees in their efforts to achieve the organization's goals?
5. In what ways are employees held accountable for achieving goals in your organization?

CHAPTER 8

Using Delegation to Your Advantage

IT'S A NEW WORLD OUT THERE . . .

Delegation and . . .

How it helps managers to get things done through others.

How delegation can make you a more effective manager.

The good and the bad of delegation.

An easy method of delegation.

Things you should and shouldn't delegate.

Keeping in touch with those to whom you delegate.

THE POWER OF DELEGATION

No manager is an island; it takes the work of a team of people—all working toward common goals—for an organization to achieve great things. So, despite the urge to try to do everything in an organization, effective managers know they can achieve far more—faster and more efficiently—by assigning specific tasks to their employees. Managers assign the responsibility for completing tasks through *delegation.*

But simply assigning tasks and then walking away is not enough. For delegation to be effective, managers must also give employees both the authority and the resources necessary to complete tasks effectively. One key measure of a manager's effectiveness lies in the ability to get things done through other people—a prime ingredient for success. And an inability to delegate undermines your effectiveness as a manager more than anything else, short of embezzlement or physical abuse.

Skillful delegation is a win-win activity. By being a good delegator, you prepare yourself for promotions and train someone who could take your place so you can move up. By delegating, others do much of the day-to-day work in your organization, freeing you up to manage, plan, and take on the kinds of jobs that only you can do as a manager. Not only that, but as your employees develop a broader range of skills as a result of having tasks delegated to them, they are likely to be more satisfied and ready to move up the organization with you. This, in turn, builds trust, enhances your career potential, and improves your organization's bottom line.

Delegation skills can make or break a manager's career. Effective delegation produces managers who, rather than being overloaded, are able to take on larger jobs in the organization and are more satisfied and better paid than those managers who don't delegate effectively.

So why do so many managers have such a hard time delegating? As you might imagine, there are a variety of reasons, including:

- They are too busy and just don't have enough time.
- They don't trust their employees to complete their assignments correctly or on time.
- They don't know how to delegate effectively.

Still not convinced that delegation is the right way to go? Okay. Consider the following list of reasons why delegation is all that—and more:

- *Your success as a manager depends on it.* The fundamental job of a manager is to get things done through others. When you're doing everything yourself, you're not getting things done through others—and you're setting yourself up for failure in a very big way.
- *You can't do it all.* We suspect that unless you live in a cartoon universe, you aren't Superman and you're not Wonder Woman. You cannot do everything yourself—it's just not possible, and you shouldn't even try.
- *Your job is to concentrate your efforts on the things that you can do and your staff can't.* As a manager, there are certain tasks that you are uniquely qualified to do, whether it's reviewing and approving budgets, pulling together a sales conference, or heading up a group of industry leaders on a trip to China. It's best for you to focus on doing your job, while you let your employees do theirs.
- *Delegation gets workers in the organization more involved.* Employees who are not allowed to play a role in the decisions that most closely affect them are employees who disengage from their organizations—going through the motions until they either quit (in favor of a company that does allow them to be involved) or retire. By delegating tasks to workers, you'll keep them engaged in their organizations—making them more effective employees in the process.

- *Delegation gives you the chance to develop your employees.* Every employee needs opportunities to learn new things and take on new tasks if they hope to progress in the organization and gain new responsibilities and promotions. What better way to help your employees develop their career skills than by delegating tasks to them? Not only do you win, but so do your employees.

DELEGATION MYTHS

Some managers avoid delegating tasks and responsibility because they have become believers in any number of common delegation myths. The following myths are just that—myths—and you shouldn't let them get in the way of your delegation efforts.

Myth 1: You Can't Trust Your Employees to Be Responsible

What? You don't trust your employees? If that's the reason you're not delegating, then you've got a real problem on your hands. The problem is that you've either hired the wrong people, or you're a perfectionist who will never be satisfied with *anything* your employees do.

In the first instance, is there any hope of either training the employees you've got and increasing their skills to a level sufficient to allow you to trust them? Or should you fire or reassign them and bring employees who can perform at a high enough level? That is a question that only you can answer, but it's one that you will need to address immediately.

In the second instance, while perfectionism can help your organization deliver better products and services, it can make things awfully tough for the employees who can't seem to avoid making the occasional mistake. If you are being too hard on your employees, then you need to start with yourself and either try to loosen up and learn that your employees are going to do the best job possible, or find someone else to run your area.

Myth 2: When You Delegate, You Lose Control of a Task and Its Outcome

Yes, it's true. When you delegate, you do lose control of how a task is done. That's the nature of delegation. You assign a task and you trust that person to get it done. But what you don't lose when you delegate is the outcome. You can agree with an employee, for example, to come up with a new system for tracking maintenance orders—that's the outcome. But how the employee comes up with the system—and how the system will ultimate work—is up to the employee to decide.

There are many different ways to get a task done—this is true both for tasks that are spelled out in highly defined steps and for tasks that are much less rigid. Instead of worrying about how your employees are going to accomplish the tasks you delegate to them, instead worry about whether the agreed outcomes are being achieved.

Myth 3: You're the Only One Who Has All the Answers

The moment your company employs more than one person, there's no way that one person—even you—can have all the answers. Your employees—working on the front line, talking to your customers, your suppliers, and one another—deal with an amazing array of situations every day. Many of these employees may have been working for the company far longer than you, and many of them will probably be there long after you're gone. They have answers too.

Myth 4: You Can Do the Work Faster by Yourself

Sure, you might very well be able to complete some specific task faster and more accurately than an employee. But if you'll just take a moment when you delegate the task, and give your employee some direction and training, it won't be long before she is able to do it as well as you. And, not only will you have more time to devote to your other duties, but your employees will have a golden opportunity to develop their work skills.

Myth 5: Delegation Dilutes Your Authority

Actually, delegation extends your authority by pushing it out over a much wider group of people. When you've got a team of employees working toward your common goals, your authority is extended—not diminished. The more authority you give to employees, the more authority your entire work unit will have and the better able your employees will be to do the jobs you hired them to do.

Myth 6: The Company Recognizes Your Employees for Doing a Good Job and Not You

Are you afraid that your employees might steal the spotlight away from your accomplishments if you delegate some of your duties and authority to them? If so, letting go of this belief may be one of the biggest difficulties for you to overcome in delegating tasks to your employees. Smart managers know that when their employees look good, they look good, too. The more you delegate, the more opportunities you give your employees to look good (and the more opportunities you give yourself to look good). When your employees do well, give your employees credit for their successes publicly and often, and others (including your boss, and your boss's boss) will notice—scoring you major points as a result, which wouldn't be such a bad thing, would it?

Myth 7: Delegation Decreases Your Flexibility

Again, the more people you delegate tasks to, the more flexibility you actually will have—not less. You can decide who to assign tasks to, who is best suited to take on certain tasks, and what tasks get priority. If something has to be done quickly, you can throw an entire team at it. There's only one of you, and if you get tied up juggling a bunch of tasks, you're not going to be very flexible when it's time to deal with those surprise problems and opportunities that always seem to pop up at the last minute.

Myth 8: Your Employees Are Too Busy

Yes, your employees might be busy, but what are they busy doing? If a task is important enough to warrant your attention, then it's important enough to be placed on your employees' priority lists. Don't just delegate tasks willy-nilly; be sure to explain their place in the big scheme of things and help your employees set their priorities. But once you've got that settled, then stand back and get out of their way. You might be surprised just how quickly—and how vigorously—they'll take care of their new duties once they are assigned.

Remember: Delegation can be scary. The more you do it, however, the less scary it gets. Your first attempts at doing some serious delegation is sort of like skydiving for the very first time: You jump out of that airplane thousands of feet above the ground and hope that the parachute opens to slow down your fall. Your employees may be a little nervous, too, so be sure to offer them more support as they discover how to become comfortable with their new roles.

DELEGATION IN SIX EASY STEPS

The delegation process is a fairly simple—and, daresay—painless one. Here are the six steps to effective delegation:

Step 1: Communicate the task. Describe exactly what you want done, when you want it done, and what end results you expect.

Step 2: Furnish context for the task. Explain why the task needs to be done, its importance in the overall scheme of things, and possible complications that may arise during its performance.

ASK BOB AND PETER: What should I do? Every day I have to tell my employees to do the same things, time after time. They can't seem to think to do these things themselves. Now they think that I'm a tyrant.

You have fallen into the micromanagement trap. While you may feel you have no choice but to tell your employees what to do every day, the result is that your employees will naturally resist your efforts and do increasingly less on their own. To solve this problem, step back for a minute and focus on your employees instead of the tasks that they can't seem to remember to do. Meet with your employees and discuss the overall goals you have for your organization; then ask them what they can do to help achieve these goals and what you can do to help them. Encourage your employees to speak up and to bring up any issues that are interfering with their ability to carry out their tasks. And when they do what you want them to do, praise them generously.

Step 3: Determine standards. Agree on the standards that you plan to use to measure the success of a task's completion. Be sure that these standards are realistic and attainable.

Step 4: Grant authority. Grant employees the authority necessary to complete assigned tasks without constant roadblocks or challenges from other employees.

Step 5: Provide support. Determine the resources necessary for your employee to complete the task and then provide him or her. Successfully completing a task may require money, training, or other resources—be sure to plan for them in advance of assigning new tasks, not after.

Step 6: Get commitment. It's not enough to make an assignment, you've also got to make sure that your employee has accepted the assignment. Confirm your expectations and the employee's under-standing of and commitment to completing the task before moving on to other matters.

Delegation benefits both workers and managers when done cor-rectly. So why not delegate more work to your employees? Jump in, the water's fine.

TASKS YOU SHOULD ALWAYS DELEGATE

There are some tasks that are best delegated to others; as a manager, you should delegate the following kinds of work to your employees whenever possible:

- *Detail work:* There's an old saying that 20 percent of the results come from 80 percent of the work. So, wouldn't it be better if the 80 percent of the effort that goes into that 20 percent of results be accomplished by your employees (who coincidentally, probably cost your company far less than you do) instead of you? Remember: you're now being paid to orchestrate the workings of an entire team of workers toward a common goal—not to do the work yourself. Leave the detail of how the work gets done to your employees, but hold them accountable for the results.
- *Information gathering:* While you might enjoy surfing the Web, reading all the business magazines and newspapers, and watching the cable financial channels—all in the name of keeping tabs on your competition—you'll be much more effective as a manager if you let someone else gather needed information. This will free you up to analyze the inputs and information and to devise solutions to your problems—and strategies for your opportunities.
- *Repetitive assignments:* You know the common sentiment, "Been there, done that." This sentiment should be your personal motto when it comes to deciding what responsibilities to delegate to

employees. Every manager should be familiar with how everything in his or her department works, and be prepared to jump in if needed in a crisis. But once you're familiar with how different tasks or responsibilities are carried out, then it's time to move on to something else. Give repetitive assignments to your employees; avoid doing them yourself.

- *Surrogate roles:* When is the last time you turned down an invitation to attend a meeting in person, but sent someone in your place instead? As a manager, this is something you should be doing much more of, not less. Not only can you not be everywhere at once, but also getting stretched too thin by commitments outside of your control does nothing to enhance your ability to manage effectively. It in fact degrades it. Whenever possible, let your employees fill in for you at presentations, conference calls, client visits, and meetings. You may be required to attend (off-site management meetings, for example), however, in many other cases, whether you attend personally or send someone in your place really doesn't matter. The hour or two you save may be your own.

AVOID DELEGATING SOME TASKS

Just as some tasks should always be delegated, others are part and parcel of the job of being a manager and should be closely held. By delegating the following work, you are avoiding your most basic management duties (and may be found superfluous the next time a layoff occurs at your company):

- *Long-term vision and goals:* Managers have a unique perspective on the organization's needs—the higher up a manager is in an organization, the broader her perspective. Although employees at any level of a company can help to shape your perspectives, developing an organization's long-term vision and goals is really up to you. This

ASK BOB AND PETER: I'm a consultant for a family-owned company. The owner/manager believes he is a superman and that he can solve any problem. Actually, he is the problem. What should I do?

There are two separate aspects of your question that can create problems for you as a consultant to this company. First, the owner/manager may not have the ability to solve the company's problems, despite the fact that he believes he can. The fact that you are there in a consultant role indicates that he needs help. We suggest you isolate the problem and develop a list of recommendations to solve the problems and ask the owner/manager to put them into effect—even if only for a trial period. Measure the quantitative improvements that result from implementing the recommendations and present them to the owner/manager. The positive results should quickly bring him around to your way of thinking. Second, the owner/manager may not understand that he is a part of the problem. This is obviously a very delicate situation, and it requires much tact to present in a way that will create positive change for the client instead of a defensive and emotional reaction against you personally. As a consultant, it's your job to tell your client problems you have found and your recommendations for solving them, as well as the positive benefits—increased employee productivity, reduced costs, increased production, improved profits, and so forth—that will result from a change in the owner/manager's management style. Your client may very well not know that he is the problem, and his employees may not want to get on his bad side by telling him so. As a consultant, you can provide an honest, outsider's opinion that he wouldn't otherwise get inside his company.

is one case where having too many people stirring the pot will get you a big mess.

- *Recognizing positive performance:* Employee rewards and recognition have the most impact when they come from an employee's manager. When this task is delegated to lower level employees, the impact of the recognition is significantly lessened and the positive effect on employee performance is greatly attenuated.

- *Performance appraisals, discipline, and counseling:* Some kinds of employee feedback have to come from managers, and this is definitely the case with performance appraisals, discipline, and counseling. When you discipline and counsel your employees, you're giving them the kind of input that only you can provide. Not only that, but such matters are highly confidential—if employees feel that their dirty laundry is hanging out where everyone can see it, trust between employees and managers will be broken. Believe us: This is one task that you can't delegate away.

- *Politically sensitive situations:* Every organization has its own unique political sensitivities, issues that are potentially highly explosive if they become known to the general population of employees. If such issues are within your own area, then putting your employees in the middle of the line of fire in a potentially explosive situation is unfair. As a manager, you're paid to make the difficult decisions and to take the political heat that your work generates.

- *Personal assignments:* Sometimes managers need to assign tasks to specific people with the intention that those people are to personally perform them. The chosen employees may have unique perspectives that no one else in the organization has; they may have unique skills that need to be brought to bear to complete the assignment quickly and accurately.

- *Confidential or sensitive circumstances:* Managers generally have access to mountains of confidential information such as wage and salary figures, proprietary data, and personnel assessments. For a variety of reasons, the unintended release of this information to the wrong individuals—whether within or without the organization—could be very damaging. Unless your staff has a compelling reason to know or work with the confidential or sensitive information, you should retain assignments involving these types of information yourself.

WHEN DELEGATION GOES WRONG

Unfortunately, despite the best of intentions, delegation goes wrong—very wrong. How can you tell if you've got a problem with delegation? The secret is to keep tabs on the tasks you delegate—and the people you delegate to—by using any or all of the following techniques:

- *Personal follow-up:* Personally visit your employees and check their progress on a regular basis.
- *Sampling:* Periodically review samples of your employees' work and check to make sure that it meets the standards you agreed to.
- *Progress reports:* Require regular progress reports from employees that can give you advance notice of problems and successes.
- A *formalized tracking system:* Create a formal system (for example, a calendar or specialized project management tracking software) to track assignments and due dates.

Sometimes your employees are going to have problems with the tasks you delegate to them. There are a variety of options for getting them and their tasks back on track:

- *Increase monitoring:* Devote more time monitoring the employees who are in trouble, keeping very close track of their performance.
- *Counsel:* Openly and frankly discuss the problems with your employees and agree on plans to correct them.
- *Rescind authority:* If problems can't be resolved in a reasonable period of time, you always have the option of rescinding your employees' authority to complete the tasks independently.
- *Reassign activities:* When delegation goes wrong, and if your employees just can't accomplish their assigned tasks, reassign them to workers who are better suited to perform them successfully.

THE REAL WORLD

The essence of managing is getting work done through others. This does not mean being a workaholic or a super problem solver, but rather to find and perfect ways to leverage the investment you and your organization have in the talent that has been hired. A poor delegator dumps work on employees, often with inadequate explanation and consideration and unrealistic time frames. A good delegator frames the work and both challenges and encourages an employee to best be able to achieve the desired results. The latter manager is clear about what needs to be done, but flexible in how the employee gets the work completed, thereby allowing for that person to have a say and imprint in his or her own work. This is an important element of effective delegation. As *Poor Richard's Almanac* puts it, "If you ride a horse, sit close and tight. If you ride a man, sit easy and light."

MONITORING PROGRESS

It's not enough to simply delegate a task and go away; managers must also monitor the results of the delegation to ensure that the tasks are being performed correctly and on time. We're not suggesting that you micro-manage your employees' every move; what we're suggesting is that although you have delegated tasks, *you* are still responsible for their satisfactory completion. It's in your interest, as well as the interest of your organization and the people within it to ensure that assigned tasks are being performed well.

Each of your employees is unique. A tight style of monitoring may work with one employee, while a loose style of monitoring may work with another. New or inexperienced employees naturally require more attention and handholding than employees who are seasoned at their jobs, and you should factor this into your monitoring style. Experienced employees who have earned high levels of trust simply don't need the kind of day-to-day attention that less experienced employees do. In fact, experienced employees may resent a manager's attempts to closely monitor the way in which they carry out their duties.

Here are some tips for monitoring delegation:

- *Tailor your approach to the employee.* If your employee works independently and is able to perform his or her job with minimal supervision on your part, establish a system of monitoring with only a few, critical checkpoints along the way. If, however, your employee needs more of your attention, create a system that incorporates several measurable milestones along the way to goal completion.

- *Diligently use a written or computer-based system for tracking the tasks that you assign to your employees.* The system you use for tracking assigned tasks doesn't matter so much as the fact that you must use the system regularly. Managers successfully use a variety of systems to track delegated tasks, including daily planners, personal digital assistants, or project management software programs.

- *Keep the lines of communication open.* Open communication is critical when it comes to delegating tasks—it is the foundation on which managers and employees build trust. Make time for your employees when they come by to ask you for help and ensure they know that you want them to come to you when there is a problem. Avoid the temptation to punish employees when something goes wrong—this often has the unintended consequence of employees hiding problems until it is too late to easily fix them.

- *Follow through on the agreements that you make with your employees.* Delegation requires trust—trust on the manager's part that an employee is going to perform an assigned task as agreed, and trust on the employee's part that the manager will provide necessary authority and support. Just as you expect your employees to follow through on their agreements with you, you must also follow through on your agreements with them. Anything less will erode the trust that is essential to building a high-performing team.

- *Reward performance that meets or exceeds your expectations, and counsel performance that falls below your expectations.* When employees do what they are supposed to do, then reward them for it. If you fail to let your employees know when they fail to meet your expectations, chances are that they will continue to fail to meet your expectations. And remember the old saying: Praise in public and criticize privately.

─────────────── **POP QUIZ!** ───────────────

Delegation is the number one way for managers to get things done in their organizations. Reflect for a few moments on what you have learned in this chapter; then ask yourself the following questions:

1. What things do you delegate to your employees?
2. What additional things *should* you delegate to your employees?
3. How do you go about getting feedback on the things that you delegate to your employees?
4. In what ways are employees held accountable for the tasks that you delegate to them?
5. In what ways do you support your employees after you delegate tasks to them?

CHAPTER 9

Monitoring Employee Performance

IT'S A NEW WORLD OUT THERE . . .

Monitoring and . . .

How employee performance can be tracked and improved.

Understanding what to measure (and how).

Important indicators of performance.

Necessary tools for monitoring employee performance.

Understanding what to do with the results.

IS YOUR ORGANIZATION PERFORMING?

It's one thing to set goals—most managers know that this is an extremely important part of their jobs—but it's another thing altogether to ensure that employees are making progress toward the successful completion of the goals they have been assigned. An organization's overall performance depends on each individual who works within it, so monitoring employee performance is a critical skill for every manager today.

But measuring and monitoring the performance of individuals in your organization is a real balancing act: On one hand you don't want to overmeasure or overmonitor your employees—detracting from their work. And, on the other hand, you don't want to undermeasure or undermonitor your employees. A failure to monitor employee performance can lead to nasty surprises when a task is completed late, over budget, or not at all—nasty surprises that will do little to enhance your career.

As a manager, your primary goal in measuring and monitoring your employees' performance should be to help your employees stay on schedule and find out whether they need additional support, not to punish them. But remember: Many employees are reluctant to admit they need help getting an assignment done. You'll therefore need systems in place to obtain the feedback you'll need on a regular basis.

IDENTIFYING KEY PERFORMANCE INDICATORS

Before you can check your employees' progress, however, you've got to determine the key indicators of a goal's success. By quantifying employee goals in precise numerical terms, your employees (and you) will be clear about how their performance will be measured and when their job performance is acceptable (or less than acceptable). Consider this example: If you define a key performance in terms of the quantity of funding applications processed per hour, your workers know exactly what you mean. The goal might be to process 25 applications per hour, with one mistake or less. Given that clear goal, your employees will quickly realize that processing only 15 applications per hour with five mistakes is unacceptable performance.

So, how do you decide what measures you'll use to monitor the progress of your employees toward completion of their goals? The answer to this question depends on the nature of the goals themselves. Some goals, for example, can be measured in terms of time, others in terms of units of production, and others in terms of final delivery of a particular work product such as a report that details the results of a competitive analysis for the introduction of a new product.

Here are some examples of goals and the different ways they can be measured:

- *Goal:* Design and implement a monthly sales report before the end of the first quarter of the current fiscal year.
  Measurement: The specific date (e.g., March 31) that the report is first mailed out (time).
- *Goal:* Increase the quantity of catalog orders processed by each employee from 100 to 125 per day.
  Measurement: The exact number of catalog orders processed by the employee each day (quantity).
- *Goal:* Increase product revenue by 20 percent in fiscal year 2009.
  Measurement: The total percentage increase in revenue from January 1 through December 31, 2009 (percentage increase).

Remember that while it's important to acknowledge and reward employees who meet their goals, it's also important to acknowledge and reward employees who are making steady progress toward meeting goals. For example:

- The goal for your line cooks is to avoid food wastage. You might encourage them by posting a large, personally signed thank-you card to your cooks on the employee bulletin board.
- The goal of your property clerks is to increase the average number of inventory transactions from 50 per day to 75 per day. You might consider publicly posting a summary of employees' daily transaction counts at the end of each week while praising these employees in your weekly department staff meeting.
- The goal for your automobile service representatives is to improve the percentage of "excellent" responses on customer feedback cards by 20 percent. You might consider keeping track of the monthly counts for each service representative and then buy lunch for the rep with the highest total for the month.

Performance measuring is built on a firm foundation of positive feedback. When employees receive positive feedback from their managers for progress made toward achieving a goal, they will be encouraged to work that much harder to achieve it. Giving negative feedback, on the other hand, may backfire. When you give negative feedback by pointing out errors, mistakes, and so on, you are making the mistake of discouraging the behaviors that you don't want when you should really be encouraging the behavior you want. Consider these examples:

- *Instead of measuring this:* number of defective printers,
  Measure this: number of correctly assembled printers.
- *Instead of measuring this:* number of weeks late,
  Measure this: number of weeks on time.
- *Instead of measuring this:* quantity of broken widgets,
  Measure this: quantity of intact widgets.

Here's a common question that most managers grapple with: Should the feedback that you provide to employees regarding their performance be public or private?

Truth be told, the results will be better when you put group performance measures (total revenues, average days sick, etc.) out in the open for everyone to see, but keep individual performance measures (sales performance by employee, tardiness rankings by employee, etc.) private. You want your team to work together to improve its performance. By tracking and publicizing group measures—and then rewarding improvement—you can get the performance you seek.

Do *not* embarrass your employees or subject them to ridicule by other employees by putting their individual performance out for everyone to see. If there are problems with individual performance, counsel and coach employees privately, and provide additional training and support, as necessary.

OBTAINING IMMEDIATE PERFORMANCE FEEDBACK

It's up to you and your employees to decide what you measure and the values that you measure against. When designing a system for measuring and monitoring your employees' performance, consider modeling it after MARS: *milestones, actions, relationships,* and *schedules,* as detailed in the following sections.

Setting Your Checkpoints: The Milestones

Goals need a starting point, a finishing point, and points in between that reflect progress from start to finish. *Milestones* are the key events and markers that tell you and your employees how far along you are on the road to reaching the goals that you've established.

Consider the goal of finalizing a new product labeling design in two months. The second milestone along the way to your ultimate goal might be having a draft sketch available for review no later than February 1. If the draft sketch is not submitted until after February 1, you'll know that the project is running behind schedule. If the sketch is submitted before February 1, you'll know that the project is on the road to early completion.

Reaching Your Checkpoints: The Actions

Actions are the individual activities that your employees perform to get from one milestone to the next. To get to the second milestone in the product label design project, your employees will need to complete several actions. These actions might include:

- Track down and review customer focus group reports.
- Meet with product manager to get her input.
- Meet with product marketing manager to get his input.
- Conduct brainstorming meeting with graphics staff.
- Create at least five draft sketches of new labels.
- Schedule meeting to present designs to management.

As you can see, each one of these actions moves everyone a little bit closer to the second milestone—completion of a draft sketch by February 1. It's important to put milestones and actions in writing and to track them methodically.

Sequencing Your Activity: The Relationships

Relationships—how milestones and actions interact with one another—shape the proper sequencing of activities that lead you to the successful, effective accomplishment of your goals. Performing certain actions before others can sometimes make achieving milestones easier, faster, and less costly. In the above list of actions, for example, it does not make sense to create the minimum of five draft sketches before obtaining feedback from the product and marketing managers. Doing so could result in substantial rework when you find out that the product manager is dead set against using the kinds of ideas that are at the heart of the draft sketches that your department has produced.

Establishing Your Time Frame: The Schedules

Finally, putting your plan into action requires the development of a *schedule* showing anticipated completion dates of the individual actions in your plan. The dates you select will result from some combination of your previous experience doing similar tasks, combined with anything new that may impact the project. Many managers find it useful to pad schedules with a little extra time here and there to allow for unanticipated problems or delays. For example, in our product label sketch project, you might expect that you'll be able to obtain feedback from the product manager within a few days, but schedule one week in the event the product manager is too busy doing other things to give your project her immediate attention.

The goals that you'll measure and monitor result from the application of each characteristic—milestones, actions, relationships, and schedules. If goals can't be measured and monitored, how will you know if you and your staff have achieved them?

PUTTING IT INTO PRACTICE

Theory is nice, but practice is better. Each of the following real-life cases demonstrates how measuring and monitoring happens in the real world. What lessons can you apply in your own organization?

Case 1: World-Class Performance

Before Bob started his own company, Nelson Motivation, Inc., he was put in charge of his previous employer's product customization department. When Bob came on board, the department was in shambles—project management was haphazard at best, with no clear system of organization, and customers had to wait weeks or even months to receive their customized products, which often came to them with countless errors. Bob was given the task of straightening the mess out.

Ask Bob and Peter: How do you handle difficult employees?

Handling difficult employees can be a real challenge for any manager, regardless of how experienced he or she is. Managers probably spend 80 percent of their staff management time dealing with the problems of only 20 percent of their workers—the ones who are the most difficult and troubled. Unfortunately, there is really little you can do about an employee's personality. It has taken years—decades, really—for an employee to develop his or her unique attitudes and quirks. The simple answer is that you're not going to change all of that history overnight. Our advice is to focus less on the subjective issue of your employees' personalities and more on the objective issue of their performance. Sure, we all want to work with pleasant people, but ultimately it is their performance that counts. If a difficult employee brought $1 billion of revenue into your company every year, we suspect you wouldn't be very upset about his or her behavior anymore. So, rather than trying to create new personalities for your difficult or high-need employees, focus your efforts on monitoring and tracking their performance instead. If it's not up to snuff, act quickly to counsel them and work out a plan for bringing performance up to acceptable levels. If they still can't hack it, you have an objective basis for making a transfer or termination.

The first thing Bob did after reviewing the department's operations and collecting data from internal and external customers was to develop a checklist of tasks to bring the organization up to a world-class level of performance. At the center of Bob's plan was a complete overhaul of the department's system for measuring and monitoring employee performance.

Step 1: Set goals with employees. After Bob drafted a checklist of what he wanted to accomplish, he talked with the employees in his new department and interviewed the department's customers—both inside and outside the organization. Bob quickly filled seven pages with negative comments about the department, work processes, finished products, and more. On his first day in the office, Bob got to witness a typical problem first hand when a company salesperson called in some urgently needed changes to one of the projects—completed the day before—only to find out that the software version of that particular product was lost. Bob figured out exactly what was interfering with his employees' ability to do a good job and then he discussed department needs and changes with them. Everyone agreed on a set of mutually acceptable goals and a game plan and—together—Bob and his employees set the stage for the next step in achieving world-class performance.

Step 2: Change the performance-monitoring system. When Bob took a look at his new department's performance reporting systems, he realized that the measures were all negative: late projects, number of mistakes, backlogged orders, and so on. There was plenty of tracking of negative performance measures, but no tracking of positive performance measures. Bob installed a new system that focused on only one performance measure—a positive one—the number of on-time projects. This changed everything. When Bob took over, the department could count only a few on-time projects. Within two years after putting this new performance measurement system into place, his department accomplished 2,700 on-time projects—a night-and-day difference.

Step 3: Revise the plan. As department performance improved, Bob implemented other improvements as well: 24-hour project quotes, project indexing, software storage, streamlining of royalty and invoicing systems, and more. Soon, the company's top management team noticed what was going on in Bob's department and liked what they saw. The department was routinely completing 80 percent of its projects within two weeks after receipt, and the

---

THE REAL WORLD

"If you can't measure it, you can't manage it" is one of the classic truisms of management. We can add to this the fact that if you can measure it, but don't, you are likely not to get the results you hoped for. A key part to being a professional manager is to make things happen according to a plan. If a plan is created, but then filed away never to be looked at until the end of the year, it is worthless. Your plans need to be living documents with action steps and deadlines. As the saying goes, "A goal is a dream with a deadline." And every deadline should have milestones that lead up to the final success.

---

customization function went from being a liability that the company's salespeople refused to use to becoming a leading competitive advantage for the company.

Case 2: Helping Your Employees Give 100 Percent

Because of ongoing performance problems, management at Cascades Diamond, Inc. in Thorndike, Massachusetts, decided to survey its employees. The results showed that 79 percent of employees felt they weren't being rewarded for a job well done, 65 percent felt that management treated them disrespectfully, and 56 percent were pessimistic about their work. With the evidence clearly in front of them, management took the following steps to fix the company's problems:

Step 1: Create a program based on the behaviors you want. Cascades Diamond's management team chartered a new club in the company, the 100 Club, to encourage and reinforce these particular behaviors:

- Attendance.
- Punctuality.
- Safety.

Points were awarded to employees based on certain measurable criteria related to these behaviors. After accumulating 100 points, employees received a special award—a nylon jacket with the Cascades Diamond logo and the words "The 100 Club" imprinted on it.

Step 2: Assign points to the desired behaviors. Employees received 25 points for a year of perfect attendance but, for each full or partial day of absence, points were deducted from their totals. Employees who went an entire year without formal disciplinary actions received 20 points, and employees who worked for a year without injuries resulting in lost time received 15 points. Employees could also receive points for making cost-saving suggestions, safety suggestions, or participating in community service projects such as Red Cross blood drives or the United Way. Management made sure that the number of points was proportionate to the behavior's importance to the organization and that the numeric goals weren't impossible to reach or demotivating.

Step 3: Measure and reward employee performance. Measuring and rewarding desired employee behavior were at the heart of Cascades Diamond's program. It was the job of supervisors and managers to closely track the performance of employees and assign points for each of the factors. When employees reached the coveted 100-point level, they were inducted into the 100 Club, and the jacket was theirs.

Of course, results speak louder than words. In the program's first year, Cascades Diamond saved $5.2 million, increased productivity by nearly 15 percent, and reduced quality-related mistakes by 40 percent. Not only that, but 79 percent of employees said that their work quality concerned them more now than before the program started, 73 percent reported that the company showed concern for them as people, and 86 percent of employees said that the company and management considered them to be either "important" or "very important." Quite a change in employee attitudes, to say the least.

TOOLS FOR WORLD-CLASS MONITORING

The measurement system you select will be simpler or more complex based on how simple or complex the performance to be measured. If the goal is simply to increase the number of customer grades of "excellent" for your customer service staff from 500 per month to 600 per month, then a simple count will tell you whether your employees have achieved the goal. However, if the goal is to design and fabricate a cold fusion reactor in one year, your job of designing a system for measuring performance will be much more difficult.

Graphical representations—Gantts, PERTs, and the like—of all the goals, milestones, actions, and schedules involved in a project are often much easier to understand than text-based lists of these items, especially for complex or prolonged projects. In the sections that follow, we'll explore some of the most common and useful.

Bar Charts

Bar charts, sometimes known as *Gantt charts,* allow managers to quickly see exactly where the project is at any given date and compare actual progress with planned progress.

Bar charts contain three basic elements:

1. *Timeline:* This is the scale by which you measure progress. The timeline can be illustrated with any units that work best for your projects, including days, weeks, months, or more. The timeline appears along the horizontal axis (the *x-axis*) in most bar charts.

2. *Actions:* These are the individual activities that must be performed to get from one milestone to the next. In a bar chart, actions are listed—usually in chronological order—vertically along the left side of the chart (the *y-axis*).

3. *Bars:* Bars on your chart indicate the estimated length of time that a particular action should take to accomplish. Short bars represent short periods of time; long bars represent long periods of time. The bars provide a quick visual reference of complete and incomplete actions.

The advantages of the Gantt chart are its simplicity, ease of preparation and use, and low cost. While Gantt charts are generally unsuitable for large, complex projects, they are great for projects that are relatively simple.

Flowcharts

As we mentioned above, bar charts are great for simple projects, but not so great for complex projects. Why? Because they don't illustrate the sequential flow of actions in a project that are predominant in complex projects. This is where *flowcharts* come to the rescue. Like bar charts, flowcharts also have three basic elements:

1. *Actions:* Arrows indicate actions, leading from one event to the next on the flowchart until the project is completed. The arrows' primary purpose in a flowchart is to illustrate the sequential relationship of actions to one another, and their length is not necessarily proportional to the amount of time between actions.

2. *Events:* Events, represented in flowcharts by numbered circles, are used to indicate completion of a particular action.

3. *Time:* Time estimates are inserted alongside each action (arrow) in the flowchart. By following a particular path and adding up the

number of time units, you can determine the total time for the completion of an action.

Flowcharts show exactly how actions relate to one another, and the *critical path*—the actions that determine how soon that a project can be completed—can be ascertained by following the longest path in terms of time. This method of analysis is commonly known as the *Critical Path Method* (CPM).

Program evaluation and review technique (PERT) is a variation of CPM that uses statistical techniques to average a range of possible times to arrive at estimates for each action when the time to complete individual actions cannot be estimated with a high degree of certainty.

PUTTING NUMBERS INTO PRACTICE

Of course, once you have all your goals, measures, and other performance measurement tools up and running, you've got to use them to positively impact the performance of your employees. Here's how to accomplish that particular task:

- *Compare results to expectations.* Let's say that your employee has a goal to complete a report by November 1. The first question is: Was the report completed on time? As it turns out, the report was completed on October 15,—two weeks before the deadline. This particular goal was accomplished with time to spare.
- *Record the results.* Note of the results in writing—in your employee's file or in a computer-based project tracking system where you keep track of all your employees' goals and responsibilities.
- *Praise, coach, or counsel your employees.* Give your employee a reward for accomplishing the goal—a simple verbal or written

thank-you is probably sufficient. If the goal was not met, however, find out why not and what your employee will do to ensure that the goal is achieved the next time.

─────────────── **POP QUIZ!** ───────────────

Monitoring employee performance is an important tool for building high-performing organizations. Reflect for a few moments on what you have learned in this chapter; then ask yourself the following questions:

1. In what ways do you currently monitor employee performance?
2. Are your measures clear and objective?
3. How do you communicate performance measures and expectations to employees?
4. To what degree have your employees had a role in determining—and bought into—the measures used to assess their performance?
5. In what ways do you share monitoring results with your employees?

CHAPTER 10

Building Employee Accountability

IT'S A NEW WORLD OUT THERE . . .

Accountability and . . .

How managers can create an environment where employees will perform.

The link between performance appraisals and accountability.

You need a process.

Common traps in the evaluation process.

Be a partner with your employees, not an executioner.

ARE PERFORMANCE APPRAISALS OBSOLETE?

One of the goals, if not *the* most important goal, of the performance appraisal and review process is to motivate employees. Yes, we know that's not what comes to mind when most people think of their performance appraisal process, which goes to show how far afield we've gotten on this topic. At its best, the performance review process encourages employees to put forth their best effort and take initiative at work to achieve both organizational and personal goals. At its worst, the exact opposite happens and employees are made to feel unimportant, abused, and unappreciated for the job they've done. Tensions mount, feelings are bruised, and goodwill is lost.

Performance appraisals and reviews are a necessary and important part of work and, for better or worse, are a reality in most organizations. However, as many companies are learning, traditional performance appraisals fail miserably in positively influencing employee behavior. In reality, the performance appraisal process has few true supporters. Indeed, many managers feel that appraisals are ineffective—a fact that their employees would likely readily agree with.

In a traditional performance review, the manager typically meets with an employee once a year and in less than an hour (and with less than an hour's preparation), attempts to get through the necessary review forms from personnel to trigger the employee's annual raise. More typically, however, the review often focuses on a negative aspect of the employee's recent job performance—not the previous 12 months' work—and is far from an accurate reflection of the employee's job performance.

As a result, an overall dissatisfaction with this system by both the employer and the employee is reflected repeatedly in surveys and studies. Employees report feeling intimidated, defensive, short-changed, and manipulated in this process. They feel that appraisals are too infrequent and occur too far from the action they are evaluating to have any meaning. In the end, employees are often demotivated by the appraisal process. For their part, many managers dread giving appraisals and, given the choice, would (and do) skip the process altogether. In fact, some 40 percent of employees report not even receiving an annual performance review.

WHY EVALUATE PERFORMANCE?

Despite these failings, most agree that—when managed correctly—there are many valid reasons to have a performance appraisal system. An objective appraisal process focuses on employee job performance toward agreed on goals, not personality traits. It recognizes the employees' contributions toward achieving organizational goals, addresses shortcomings, identifies education needs, and is a meaningful part of a person's career planning process. For most organizations, this process is also the basis for employee compensation.

The appraisal process also helps companies make decisions about promotability, training and staffing needs, and salary and compensation benefits. And, there are many legal reasons for a well-designed, well-implemented appraisal program, including its use as legal documentation in the event of an employee termination. However, performance appraisal programs continue to receive a lot of attention in the courts, particularly in how they impact employment for protected employee groups. The legal implications for companies without a well-defined appraisal program are serious. Recent court decisions indicate that a successfully defended appraisal program includes the following:

- Specific instructions and training were given to supervisors on how to complete the appraisals.
- Job content was used to develop the basis of the appraisal.

- Appraisals were based on objective performance criteria, not on subjective personality traits.
- The results of the completed appraisal were reviewed with the appraised employee. The employee was given the opportunity to comment and submit written comments if appropriate.

So, we ask the question again: Why evaluate performance? Perhaps at the top of the list of possible answers to that question is this: Because when you evaluate employee performance—and make it a part of your organization's system of delegation, goal setting, coaching, motivating, and ongoing informal and formal feedback on employee performance—you can improve it. In addition, evaluating performance provides you with:

- *A chance to summarize past performance and establish new performance goals:* Every employee wants to know if he or she is doing a good job. If there's one thing that performance evaluations do well, it's requiring managers to take the time to sit down with employees—if only for a few minutes once a year—and talk about performance. Even better is when managers spend half an hour or more, two or more times a year, providing every employee with feedback on performance, and then setting goals for the upcoming evaluation period.
- *An opportunity for clarification and communication:* It's not uncommon for managers to think they know what employees consider to be important, while what employees actually think is important is quite different. Here's a great exercise to do with your employees: List the employee's 10 most important activities. Then ask your employee to list what he or she considers to be his or her 10 most important activities. We'll wager that your lists are quite different. Performance evaluations help you and your employees make sure that you're in agreement on assignments and priorities.

- A *forum for learning goals and career development:* Most managers make career development a key part of the performance evaluation process. Despite the fact that we advise managers to conduct career development discussions in a forum separate from the performance evaluation process, we do agree that it's better to do it during the performance evaluation process than not at all.

- A *formal documentation to promote advancement or dismissal:* When it's time to recommend someone for a promotion, or to build a case for dismissal, you're going to need written documentation to support whatever position you take. A written performance review provides you with just the kind of documentation you'll need in either case.

CREATING A PROCESS FOR EVALUATION

One of the most important things you can do as a manager is conduct accurate and timely performance evaluations of your employees. Remember: Feedback is the breakfast of champions, and its hard for your employees to get too much of it.

Many managers, however, tend to see the performance evaluation process in very narrow terms: How can I get this thing done as quickly as possible so I can get back to my real job (usually the manager's own tasks, projects, and work)? In their haste to get the evaluation done and behind them, many managers merely consider a few examples of recent performance and base their entire evaluation on them. And because few managers give their employees the kind of meaningful, ongoing performance feedback that they need to do their jobs better, the performance evaluation can become a dreaded event—full of surprises and dismay. Or it can be so sugarcoated that it becomes a meaningless exercise in management. This scenario isn't the right way to evaluate your employees.

There is much more to the performance evaluation process than simply providing a few examples of recent performance and basing their entire result on them. Follow these six steps to help you encompass the broader scope of the performance evaluation process:

Step 1: Set goals, expectations, and standards. Before you can evaluate your employees on their performance, you have to set goals and expectations with them and develop standards that you'll use to measure their performance. These goals and expectations then have to be communicated to your employees—before you evaluate them, not after. To maximize employee buy-in of the goals and expectations, make sure that employees have a voice in setting them.

Step 2: Give continuous and specific feedback. Don't save feedback only for special occasions, catch your employees doing things right and give them positive feedback on the spot. And if you need to give your employees negative feedback, then don't hesitate—try to do so as soon as you can after the performance you want corrected occurs. Your feedback will be much more effective as a result.

Step 3: Prepare a formal, written performance evaluation with your employee. Use the written evaluation forms provided, or create one of your own. The key is to be sure that the evaluation form includes a complete list of goals and expectations for the evaluation period and that these are what you'll base your evaluation on. Use lots of examples to illustrate your judgments, and keep your evaluation focused on the goals, expectations, and standards that you have already developed and communicated.

Step 4: Meet personally with your employees to discuss the performance evaluation. Employee performance evaluation meetings are much more effective when they are conducted in person instead of via mail, e-mail, or telephone. Select a location for your meeting that's comfortable and free of distractions, and be sure to make the meeting positive and upbeat. When you discuss performance problems, bring the discussion around to discussing ways that you and your employees can work together to solve them.

Step 5: Set new goals, expectations, and standards. The performance evaluation meeting is the perfect opportunity to review and discuss the things that worked well and the things that, perhaps, didn't work so well, and to set new goals, expectations, and standards for the next review period.

Step 6: Link to areas of personal development. The best performance evaluations place the job in a larger context of the employee's career and journey toward increased responsibilities in the organization. Look for opportunities for personal growth and development, and discuss strategies for helping the employee achieve those goals.

WATCHING OUT FOR EVALUATION TRAPS

Managers have to be careful not to fall into one or more of the many evaluation traps. Here's a comprehensive listing of the most common mistakes that managers make when evaluating employee performance:

- *The halo effect:* This trap occurs when a manager ignores the bad things an employee is doing because he or she is good in other areas. You might, for example, ignore for some time that an employee is the subject of numerous complaints of sexual harassment because she happens to be your top salesperson.
- *The recency effect:* It's natural for managers to most remember what employees have done most recently. An employee can be performing poorly all year, but two weeks before the performance evaluation is initiated, his performance becomes outstanding. A manager might "forget" about the months and months of poor performance

and remember only the outstanding performance that commenced only recently.

- *Stereotyping:* As hard as we try, it's hard not to believe in stereotypes or preconceived notions of how someone believes or will act. You might, for example, be certain that women make better customer service representatives than do men. This stereotyping works to give female employees higher ratings, and men lower ratings.

- *Comparing:* It's hard not to compare the performance of two or more employees who you are rating at the same time. Your high-performing employees will naturally make your lower-performing employees look bad in comparison. In the same manner, mediocre performers are going to look good when stacked up against poor performers.

- *Mirroring:* This occurs when you fall into the trap of rating highly those employees who are most like you (same likes, dislikes, interests, hobbies, and so forth) and rating lowly those employees who are least like you. While the employees who are most like you will appreciate the favor, the employees you don't favor won't.

- *Nice guy/gal:* Many managers absolutely dread conducting performance evaluations because it forces them to acknowledge the failings of their employees and then talk to their employees about those failings. Most managers would much rather give their employees good news rather than bad, but sometimes bad news is all you've got. But every manager must be prepared to give both if employees are to improve in their jobs and become more effective.

ONGOING PERFORMANCE FEEDBACK

In today's dynamic, fast-paced workforce, enlightened companies recognize that employees want an environment that encourages a constant dialogue between employer and employee. Today, employees want and need continuous performance feedback. They want to be recognized and rewarded for their accomplishments, and, at the same time, most employees want feedback if their performance is missing the mark so they can make changes as appropriate. "Men and women want to do a good job, a creative job, and if they are provided the proper environment they will do so," says Bill Hewlett, cofounder of Hewlett-Packard (quoted from *The 100 Best Companies to Work for in America* by Robert Levering, Milton Moskowitz, and Michael Katz, New York: Signet, 1984).

Employees want to know how they're performing, and they want—and need—to know more frequently than annually. "Continuous, supportive communication from managers, supervisors, and associates is too often underemphasized," says Jim Moultrup, consultant, Management Perspectives Group. "It is a major, major motivator." After all, a motivated workforce, willing to take initiative when they see the opportunity, is a powerful advantage for a company (quoted from "Success Through People: A New Era in the Way America Does Business," *Incentive*, by Aaron Sugarman, May 1988, pp. 20–24, 156–157). People want to learn new things, to feel they've made a contribution—that they are doing worthwhile work. Few people are motivated only by money. Indeed, today, a performance appraisal program that effectively motivates employees may give a company its greatest competitive advantage.

There are other less tangible, but equally important, benefits of an ongoing appraisal process. Managers increasingly must serve as coaches to influence desired behavior. *Effective* performance reviews and appraisals help strengthen the communication between a manager and an employee and foster a relationship of trust and respect to be nurtured over time. As one employee put it: "When management shows through actions rather than words that you're a valuable employee, that your input is valued no matter what level you work at, it's very motivating." Appraisals no longer need to be viewed as a necessary evil but rather as a tool that can be used to enhance your career.

Rewards and recognition also play an important role in motivating employees. While money is important to employees, what tends to *motivate* them to perform—and to perform at higher levels—is the thoughtful, personal kind of recognition that signifies appreciation for a job well done. In a recent study of more than 1,500 employees in various work settings, Dr. Gerald H. Graham, professor of management at Wichita State University, found the most powerful motivator was personalized, immediate recognition from their managers. "Managers have found that simply asking for employee involvement is motivational in itself," says Graham. The top five motivating techniques determined by Graham's study were (quoted from "The Motivational Impact of Nonfinancial Employee Appreciation Practices on Medical Technologists," *Health Care Supervisor,* by Gerald H. Graham and Jeanne Unruh, 1990, pp. 9–17):

1. The manager personally congratulates employees who do a good job.
2. The manager writes personal notes about good performance.
3. The organization uses performance as the basis for promotion.
4. The manager publicly recognizes employees for good performance.
5. The manager holds morale-building meetings to celebrate successes.

A recent survey conducted by the Minnesota Department Resources (quoted from *Recognition Redefined: Building Self-Esteem at Work,* by Roger L. Hale and Rita F. Maehling, Minneapolis, MN: The Tennant Company, 1992) supports Graham's findings in discovering that recognition activities contributed significantly to employees' job satisfaction. Most respondents said they highly value day-to-day recognition from their supervisors, peers, and team members. The survey also found:

- 68 percent of the respondents said it is important to believe that their work is appreciated by others.
- 63 percent agreed that most people would like more recognition for their work.
- 67 percent agreed that most people need appreciation for their work.

ASK BOB AND PETER: What's the most proven way of doing job evaluations and compensating employees according to the results of the evaluations?

Job evaluations are a very sensitive part of the personnel system for any company. If there is anything that will get an employee upset, it is thinking that he or she is being unfairly paid relative to other employees. There is a definite trend in many organizations toward a market-based system; that is, salaries are aligned with the comparative worth of the job in the marketplace. Within those parameters, employees need to be held to the specific performance objectives they agreed to meet since their last performance appraisal or since they accepted the position.

FEEDBACK, FEEDBACK, AND MORE FEEDBACK

Many companies have abandoned traditional appraisals in favor of a system that frequently answers one of the most urgently asked questions by employees: "How am I doing?" In an article by Gina Imperato titled "How To Give Good Feedback" in *Fast Company* magazine (Issue 17, September 1998, p. 144), Glenroy Inc., a privately held manufacturer of packaging materials outside Milwaukee, Wisconsin, held a rally at which employees built a bonfire and burned the company's manuals with their well-established approach to performance reviews. Says Michael Dean, Glenroy's executive vice-president, "Leaders here provide people with feedback. But the way for it to be effective is on a day-by-day, minute-by-minute basis—not once or twice a year." Some management experts go so far as to say that 90 percent of a manager's job today occurs in the day-to-day coaching of employees (as discussed in Chapter 5).

Enlightened companies recognize that it is the daily interactions between managers and employees that provide the greatest opportunity for valuable feedback. Employees don't want surprises—and an effective appraisal process avoids surprising employees. Too often, managers fail to seize the moment and provide timely feedback. Instead, they "save" it for the annual review discussion, and the golden opportunity to positively influence an employee's behavior when it occurs is missed.

OTHER NEEDS IN CHANGING TIMES

There are other reasons your organization should consider an emphasis on daily communication over traditional yearly performance reviews, including the prevalence of teams, alternate work arrangements, and the impact of technology.

Prevalence of Teams in U.S. Companies

Much of the work done in American companies today is accomplished through teamwork. The prevalence of teams is another major reason for companies to reassess the way in which they evaluate their employees' performance. Traditional appraisal systems were developed with only individual performance in mind and are generally not designed to evaluate performance as part of a team. Complicating the evaluation process even more is the existence of so many different types of teams with responsibility for short-term projects to projects conducted over several years. Despite this confusion, appraisal systems can, and must, be made team friendly.

Developing performance goals and objectives for the team *and* for each individual member of the team is critical to assessing the success of each. Because teams are integral to work today, measuring *both* team and individual performance is important. Linking the goals of the team and its individual members to the organization's objectives is also important. Connecting the two makes it possible to accurately recognize and reward the team and/or the individuals for their contributions to the company results. Though teams may appear to present another wrinkle in the performance appraisal system, well-defined goals and objectives, clearly communicated and supported by continual feedback and recognition for the team and its members, help ensure the team's success.

Alternative Work Arrangements

Another sign that the work world is changing is the increasing number of telecommuters, job-sharing, and off-site arrangements. For example, some 40 percent of organizations now allow employees to telecommute in some capacity. These flexible work situations are becoming more commonplace and present another challenge for companies. How do you evaluate performance, provide feedback, and motivate employees with whom you have little face-to-face contact? Because these types of work arrangements are relatively new, there is no well-established performance appraisal process by which these employees are to be evaluated. However, as companies work to develop systems to effectively address these situations, it is important that employees' need for feedback and recognition is met on a daily basis. This requires an ongoing commitment to communicate and connect with employees perhaps more than ever before.

Impact of Technology

If left unchecked, the increasing use of technology in today's business can have an alienating effect on employees. But, technology today can also offer employers many options for better communicating and connecting with their people. The key is learning how to use the technology and then taking advantage of all it can offer. Voice mail and e-mail can be effective tools for daily communication with employees—especially

---

THE REAL WORLD

For most people, *accountability* is a dirty word, suggesting they might not do what they were supposed to unless they were closely watched and perhaps even badgered to comply. The fact of the matter is, however, high performers love to be held accountable because it helps to quantify how much they are able to get done. And for everyone else, they *need* the feedback to get to become a high performer. The more employees are held accountable, the more they tend to rise to the challenge of performing. So think in terms of *positive accountability* in a way that highlights the impact of your efforts and increases dialogue and communication for everyone to be better.

---

for thanks and encouragement. A.G. Edwards, the financial services company, goes further and uses technology to conduct a weekly phone conference *of all employees.*

One step closer to face-to-face communication is the use of video-conferencing. Home Depot, for example, has a weekly satellite feed to all stores known as "Breakfast with Bernie and Arthur," its chairman and CEO. Still, when the issue for discussion is emotionally charged, it is best to schedule a face-to-face meeting as soon as possible. If that's not possible in a reasonable time, it is better to provide feedback using some form of technology than not at all.

WHAT MAKES A GOOD PERFORMANCE SYSTEM?

Performance appraisals—in the traditional sense of the term—are obsolete. To be effective, the performance review process must be updated to take into account the needs of employees and the nature of today's fast-paced business environment. To be successful, a good performance appraisal process must be participative—that is, the employee must have a voice in the process. Involving the employee in establishing goals and objectives for his or her job not only generates a sense of fairness about the process but also is an effective way to improve job performance. In addition to mutually setting employee goals and objectives, the performance process needs to link individual goals to the organization, identify education and development needs, and discuss career advancement opportunities. Done well, this process serves as an excellent foundation for the ongoing communication advocated earlier.

Providing employees with continuous feedback in a timely and nonthreatening manner is at the core of how employers can effectively motivate their employees. Employees today need and want frequent recognition of their job performance and will put forth their best effort for employers who fulfill this need. Companies that continually reward and recognize their employees in an environment of ongoing communication will create a workforce that feels empowered to make a difference.

GETTING TO THE HEART OF ACCOUNTABILITY

Accountability is something that every manager wants and expects from his or her employees but is often elusive to obtain. How are employees held accountable for the jobs they were hired to do, the results they promised to achieve, and the goals they agreed to reach? And how do managers create an environment in which employee accountability is positive, even enjoyable, and certainly valuable? For most organizations, for better or worse, this is accomplished via performance evaluations, that is, timely and accurate evaluations of an employee's successes and shortcomings.

Most managers and supervisors, however, dread doing performance evaluations, and even more employees dread receiving them. According to studies on the topic, an estimated 40 percent of all workers never receive performance evaluations. And for the 60 percent of the workers who do have reviews, most are poorly done. Very few employees receive regular, formal performance evaluations that are thoughtful, complete, and constructive to the employee.

Ask any human resources manager: Are formal performance evaluations really necessary? The answer you get will likely be a resounding "yes!" However, if you look a little below the surface, the reality may echo something quite different. Although most managers consider performance evaluations a necessary tool in developing their employees, reinforcing good performance, and correcting poor performance, these evaluations are often too little, too late. They often miss the mark as tools for developing employees. If performance evaluations are done poorly, managers are better off not doing them at all—especially if by not doing evaluations, the alternative is more frequent coaching and communication.

EVALUATE; DON'T AMBUSH

When an evaluation process is working in an organization, employees aren't surprised by the results. In such organizations, employees receive regular and ongoing feedback on their progress from their managers. Then, when it comes time to conduct a formal performance evaluation, you can focus on summarizing the things that you've previously discussed and on strategies to improve.

But, for the evaluation process to work as well as it can, managers must be fully prepared for employee evaluations. Leaving the preparation for performance evaluation meetings until the last possible minute is a prescription for disaster. The average manager spends about one hour preparing for an employee review that required an entire year of performance. This is not nearly enough time to be properly prepared for a performance evaluation meeting.

In summary, when it comes to ongoing accountability about employee performance, keep these points foremost:

- Communication with employees should be frequent so there are no surprises. You should give your employees informal feedback on their performance early and often.
- The primary focus of performance appraisals should be on going forward—setting new goals, improving future performance—rather than on looking back.
- Learning and development should always be included as a part of the performance appraisal process (although sometimes a discussion about pay raises can be separate).

The entire process consists of setting goals with your employees, monitoring their performance, coaching them, supporting them, counseling them, and providing continuous feedback on their performance—both good and bad. If you've been doing these things before you sit down for your annual or semiannual performance evaluation session with your employees, you're going to find reviews a pleasant wrap up and look at the past accomplishments instead of a disappointment for both you and your employees.

Don't be among the many managers who fail to give their employees ongoing performance feedback and, instead, wait for the scheduled review. Despite your best intentions and the best efforts of your employees, assignments can easily go astray. Schedules can stretch, roadblocks can stop progress, and confusion can wrap its ugly tentacles around a project. However, if you haven't set up systems to track the progress of your employees, you may not figure out this oversight until too late. You end up mad, and your employees get black eyes because of their mistakes.

---------------------------- POP QUIZ! ----------------------------

Holding employees accountable in their jobs is a challenging aspect of any manager's job. Consider the following questions that address topics covered in this chapter:

1. What is employee accountability, and how does a manager best get it?
2. Why are performance evaluations useful? What makes them challenging?
3. What are important prerequisites for any effective performance evaluation?
4. Name three common traps that undermine performance evaluations, and describe how to avoid each.
5. Name three ways to make performance evaluations more positive and constructive for both managers and employees.

PART

Building High-Performance Organizations

CHAPTER 11

Improving Communication

IT'S A NEW WORLD OUT THERE . . .

Communication and . . .

How good communication makes organizations work better.

How to become a better listener.

Learning how to make great presentations.

The power of the written word.

Keeping up with technology.

COMMUNICATION MAKES
ORGANIZATIONS WORK

Think about it for a minute: What would your organization be like without communication? Our guess is that it would be a very lonely place. Not only could teams not coordinate their efforts and individuals seek feedback from and communicate their successes to their managers, but also customers would have a pretty tough time placing orders, products would have a pretty tough time being produced, and services would have a pretty tough time being delivered. If you couldn't communicate with coworkers, team members, customers, suppliers, and others with whom you routinely do business, you really wouldn't have an organization at all.

In short, organizations are built on a foundation of communication; communication is the physical and mental network that ties everyone—both within and without the organization—together. It's the oil that keeps the organization running smoothly.

But, while communication is simple when an organization has only one or two people in it, the complexity of communication grows in direct proportion to the size of the organization. In larger organizations, communication occurs less in face-to-face encounters than in increasingly impersonal ways such as voice mail and e-mail messages. And, as organizations grow and its members are dispersed across town—or around the globe—communication becomes that much more difficult as distance and other obstacles impede clear and effective communication.

In every organization, the lion's share of business communication occurs in four different formats (and each format is used in greater or lesser frequency and is, therefore, more or less important to those in the organization):

1. Listening (most frequent).
2. Speaking/presenting (next most frequent).
3. Writing (next most frequent).
4. Reading (least frequent).

The greatest amount of business communication consists of listening, followed by speaking and presenting, with writing and reading bringing up the rear. That's all well and good, but guess how much training most Americans get during the course of their lives for each of these different communication formats? Surprisingly, results show that the communication formats most important in the workplace are the formats for which people get the least training:

1. Listening (little formal training offered).
2. Speaking/presenting (optional classes).
3. Writing (numerous years of term papers).
4. Reading (12+ years of systematic development).

Is it any surprise that communication in many organizations is a problem? The truth is that, although communication is critically important to the success of organizations—perhaps more so than ever before—it is often, at best, dysfunctional, and, at worst, terribly broken. In this chapter, we consider the most important communication formats within organizations and what you can do as a manager to become a better practitioner—and to help your coworkers improve their skills.

THE LOST ART OF LISTENING

As mentioned in the preceding section, listening is the most important communication format in organizations today, but it is also the format that we are least prepared for when we enter the workforce.

THE BIG PICTURE

NORWOOD DAVIS

Former chairman and CEO, Trigon Healthcare, Inc. (now Wellpoint, Inc.)

Question: How do you communicate goals effectively in a 4,000-person operation?

Answer: That is probably one of the biggest challenges there is, and I have tried to figure that out for years. And one of the most frustrating things about it is when you have a really good strategy and you think you have a pretty clear goal and you've got to rely on other people to get that across. You can't talk individually to 4,000 people. The conversion of this company to a publicly traded company gave us a great opportunity. In hindsight, we tried to be too much. We tried—this is an overstatement—to be all things to all people, and there were too many important things that we thought. We were focused on basically two things: meeting Wall Street's earnings estimates and customer service. We knew we needed not only satisfied customers, but customers that would renew with us to get the earnings in the long term. It's very well understood throughout our company that we will take whatever steps necessary to produce 15 percent earnings growth every year. We would do whatever it took to make sure we received very high levels of customer satisfaction, which we would measure through independent surveys. This business was consolidating, and we wanted to have positioned ourselves so that when the business consolidated, we would be the Mid-Atlantic and Southeast health plan of choice. There's nothing about all the other stuff you can come up with in terms of corporate goals and objectives. Those things support these goals.

Question: And then you roll this message out, right?

Answer: Well, it's not only rolling it out; it's also the actions to support it. If you're a public company, the analysts will tell you that if you miss their estimate, they'll sell the stock and then they'll call you and

(Continued)

find out why you missed the estimate because they know that if they don't sell, somebody else is going to sell. So if you think back where we were 2½ years ago, we were a mutual insurance company—a nonprofit organization. There was a lot of skepticism on Wall Street as to whether we could compete and survive during our conversion to a stock company—competing for the same capital as the established public companies were—let alone prosper in that kind of environment. We knew we would have to change the culture of the company and we did. We have the stock quote on the wall in the electronic readout in all the cafeterias.

Question: It doesn't get any more immediate than that.

Answer: We also gave all our employees stock options, which is a little bit unusual in our industry. And then we talked to them about what's going on financially with the company, what's going on with the customers. Our customer service measurements results are far better now than they were back then. It really does work.

The good news is that, with a little attention and practice, you can become a world-class listener—someone who will make even Dr. Phil jealous.

Here are some tips for becoming a better and more effective listener:

- *Be interested in the other person.* Most people are pretty perceptive, and they can tell when someone (meaning you) is interested—really interested—in what they have to say and when he or she is not. And as soon as they figure out that you aren't interested in what they have to say (because of your constant interruptions, taking phone calls during your conversation, or staring at the ceiling), they'll soon clam up, eventually not bothering to communicate with you at all. Conversely, when people know you are interested in what they have to say, they will increase their communication, which is good for you as a manager and good for the organization.

- *Be focused.* People can think more than three times faster than they can speak (500 words per minute versus 150 words per minute); this gap can lead to problems when your mind starts to wander. A wandering mind comes across to the speaker that you're not interested in what he or she has to say. The result? A shutdown of communication, which will likely be fixed only when you get focused on your subject and express your interest in what the other person has to say. Stay focused on the conversation, and you'll save yourself a lot of potential problems.

- *Ask questions.* When you ask questions, you're really doing two different things. In the first case, you're showing the speaker that you're interested in what he or she has to say. In the second case, you're ensuring that communication is clear and that you understand exactly what is being said. One technique—*reflective listening*—where you summarize what the speaker says and then repeat it to him or her, is a way of asking questions while reinforcing what the speaker has said—improving communication in the process.

- *Get to the point.* Some people, through no real fault of their own, love to hear themselves talk, and they will go on and on talking about issues that have little or nothing to do with the main point of the conversation. You can be an active listener and help the speaker get to the point by gently steering him or her away from these unimportant issues and toward the main point. If you do it right, you'll get to the heart of the issue—and be able to address it— much sooner and with a minimum of muss and fuss.

- *Avoid interruptions.* There are two kinds of interruptions that can get in the way of effective listening: interruptions that you, the listener, make and interruptions that come from others. In the first case, while you want to use active listening techniques to encourage the speaker to keep the conversation moving forward, you do not want to continually interrupt the speaker. This will simply cause the speaker to get off track or to become frustrated. In the second case, interruptions from others—such as when you stop a conversation because someone calls or because someone drops by your office—can be just as disruptive to the communication process. Respect the speaker by giving him or her your full attention.

- *Use more than your ears.* Up to 90 percent of the communication in a typical conversation is nonverbal. So, while a speaker's mouth is saying the words, his or her body is actually doing the majority of the talking. Nonverbal communication includes positions of arms, legs, and other body parts; facial expressions; overall posture; and more. Because nonverbal communication is so important, you need to use your eyes to listen as much or more as you use your ears.

MAKING PRESENTATIONS

Take another look at the list of different forms of communication at the beginning of this chapter. While listening is at the very top of the list in importance, speaking and making presentations are next on the list. Since we assume you already know how to speak, we're going to focus on the art of making effective presentations.

You've no doubt experienced the thrill of seeing talented speakers doing their thing. When speakers are *on,* they have you in the palm of their hand, bringing you into their vision and transporting you to another place. And, while a talented speaker makes presentations seem effortless, every great speaker knows that the key to giving a great presentation is to be very well prepared. Here are some tips for getting ready for your own presentations.

- *Understand exactly what it is you want to accomplish.* Why are you giving the presentation in the first place? What do you hope to accomplish during the presentation? What do you hope attendees will do after your presentation? Who will be in the audience, and what will they be hoping to gain from your presentation? Determine your goals for the presentation and the information your listeners will need to receive for you to achieve your goals.

- *Prepare your outline.* If you want to know where you're going, the best way to get there is with a map. An outline is the map that will guide you through your presentation, ensuring that you hit each of the major points that you want to communicate to your audience and the supporting data for each point. It's also a good idea to fill in subpoints under each of your major points, which further elaborate the information you want to convey. *Do not write a speech.* Reading from a written script is guaranteed to make you look stilted and dry while putting your audience to sleep. An outline provides you with the thought prompts you'll need during your presentation, allowing you to fill in the blanks yourself—making for a much more interesting presentation.

- *Write your introduction and conclusion.* Every presentation needs a beginning (introduction) and an end (conclusion). Your introduction should do three things: (1) Explain to your audience what they're going to gain from your presentation, (2) explain to your audience why the presentation is important to them, and (3) get your audience's attention. Similarly, your conclusion should also do three things: (1) Summarize your key points, (2) refer your listeners back to the introduction, and (3) inspire your audience to action. The next time you have the opportunity to experience a really good presentation, see how the speaker uses these techniques to build compelling introductions and conclusions.

- *Develop clear transitions.* Write out the transition statements that connect key points of your speech to be sure they clearly link and build on your arguments. Without clear transitions, a speaker can inadvertently leave the audience scratching their heads as the speaker takes off in a new direction in the presentation.

- *Practice, practice, practice.* The old saying really is true: Practice makes perfect. If the presentation you're making is an informal

(?) **ASK BOB AND PETER:** I manage a staff of about 24 at a German bank. Two of my analysts are Hispanic, sit next to each other, and often start speaking Spanish to each other loudly and joking around in Spanish. This makes those around them a bit uncomfortable because they do not speak the language and find it to be rude. I am Puerto Rican, so I have no problem with talking to them about this issue but would like to solicit your advice on the best way to do this, especially since two of my other analysts are German employees slotted to work for me for one year, who happen to communicate with each other in German all the time. How can I seem fair if it is permissible to me for my two German-speaking analysts to converse in German? I find it permissible because German is their primary language and because they communicate to my Frankfurt Branch in German and the bank is a German Bank. Your advice would be most appreciated.

From the information you've given us, it would appear that your organization has no rules requiring that employees speak only English in the workplace. And you're right, it really wouldn't be fair to tell the two Spanish-speaking employees that they can't speak to each other in their native tongue at the same time you allow the two German-speaking employees to do so—regardless of who owns the bank. Your consideration should be whether (1) the performance of your Spanish-speaking employees is being impacted by this practice and (2) the performance of other employees is being impacted by the practice. We suspect that there is a positive impact in the first case and perhaps a small negative impact in the second. Regardless of what language your employees speak, if their behavior is disruptive to other employees (speaking loudly and constant joking), you should counsel them to tone it down. We would advise against an outright prohibition of speaking Spanish at work. You not only negatively impact the morale of the two Spanish-speaking employees but also open yourself up to a claim of discrimination if you don't also ban the speaking of German and other languages besides English at work.

one to your work team, you'll need little in the way of practice—you might need none at all. But if the presentation is to your board of directors or to an industry audience of 2,500 people, then putting some significant time into practice before you make your presentation is an investment that will surely pay off. To get real-time feedback, give the presentation in front of a trusted colleague, or you can videotape it and review it to see where you need to make improvements.

All this preparation has a reason: to do the very best job you can communicating your thoughts to your audience. After you've gotten prepared, it's time to present. Here are the five steps for making your presentation one that will not only accomplish your goals but also impress those who attend.

Step 1: Relax. It would be easy for us to tell you that you have no reason to be nervous, you've prepared yourself for the presentation, and your audience is looking forward to hearing what you have to say, but the reality is public speaking is a top fear for most people. The good news is that a bit of nervousness will make you a better speaker, giving your presentation an edge of excitement that it wouldn't have if your heart wasn't pumping and your knees weren't quaking. Take some deep breaths, and visualize yourself giving a great presentation. Repeat a positive affirmation such as, "I'm glad I'm here, I'm glad you're here, I know what I know, and I care about you."

Step 2: Greet your audience. One of the best ways to be relaxed during a presentation—especially a presentation before a large group of people—is to arrive early and engage members of the audience as they file into the room. Chat with them informally, asking their names, and ask what they hope to gain from the presentation. Instead of a roomful of strangers, you all of a sudden have some friends in the audience helping you to relax and feel more at ease.

Step 3: Listen to your introduction. If you're making a formal presentation before a group where someone is going to introduce you (providing the audience with a brief biography and explanation of why you're there), then pay close attention. You may be able to key off something said by the introducer or open your presentation with a humorous story or anecdote that relates to the context of the meeting.

Step 4: Get your audience's attention. Before you start your presentation, be sure that you first have your audience's attention. If someone introduces you, that automatically focuses the attention on you. If, however, you're making your presentation without an introduction, you may have to figure out a way to get a large group of people who are talking among themselves—oblivious to what is going on in the front of the room—to stop talking and to focus their attention on you. One technique is to walk up to the spot where you'll be speaking in the front of the room, and just stand there. Don't say a word. Soon, people will stop talking and start focusing on you. Only when everyone stops talking should you begin your presentation.

Step 5: Make your presentation. Here's the chance to put all your hard work and practice into action. Remember, people want to hear what you've got to say, and they want you to succeed (at least most of them do). Just stick with your plan, and everything will be all right.

PUT IT IN WRITING

Written communication is also a critical skill to master in most any professional job since so much communication—memos, e-mail messages, reports, and the like—are in writing. And, as anyone who has unintentionally hurt the feelings of a coworker because of a too-hastily drafted e-mail knows, the ability to craft well-written documents is an important skill to possess.

THE REAL WORLD

In this day and age, there tends to be an excess of information, but often a lack of true communication. In fact, the more *connected* we have become electronically (with cell phones, pagers, Palm Pilots, voice mail, e-mail, faxes, etc.), the less *connection* we seem to really have with others today. We have become skilled at processing. Sometimes through all this clutter and information overload, the best communication comes from a 100 percent dedicated focus on a person and the issue being discussed. As Roy Moody of Roy Moody Associates once said: "The most motivating thing one person can do for another is to listen." To listen *naively*, that is, without an agenda or thinking about your response, is a vital skill that we all need to work at every day. When communication is really lacking, it is sometimes best to "metacommunicate," that is, to talk about the process of communication and how it can be improved for everyone's benefit.

What are some of the best ways to improve your writing skills? As writers ourselves, we have assembled some of the best in the following list.

- *Organize.* Before you start to write, organize your thoughts. This can be accomplished in a variety of different ways. Some people find that sketching out an outline of major points works to improve their writing, while others find that simply taking time to visualize the final written product does the trick. Whatever your approach, the better organized you are before you start to write, the better will be the finished product.

- *Write like you speak.* Formal, stilted memos and documents are out; informal, accessible written communications are in. While businesses once put a premium on formality in communication, this is no longer the case. Rather than spending hours crafting the grammatically perfect memo of yore, today's businesspeople would rather jot off a quick e-mail message and use their time more effectively.

- *Make it short and sweet.* Get to the point quickly, and make your points clearly. Unless the document you're working on is a technical report containing page after page of test results, there is really no valid reason to fill your written communications with page after page of words when you could have said what you wanted to say in just a couple of paragraphs. Complex, lengthy written communications often get put to the side and are never read, defeating the purpose of writing the document in the first place. But simplicity doesn't mean stupid; simplicity simply means getting to the point quickly and creating documents that everyone in your organization can read, understand, and implement. Remember, simpler is often better when it comes to putting your thoughts in writing.

- *Hone your message.* One of the secrets of great writing is the ability to edit and hone a message down to its true essence. As the rule goes, don't use 10 words when one will do. Good writers know the power of good editing and rewriting. While their first drafts may be pretty good, a good rewrite can turn a pretty good document into one that will knock your socks off. While busy businesspeople shouldn't dwell too long on their written communications, they should take some time to closely review, edit, and then rewrite their drafts so that they will have an opportunity to really shine.

- *Accentuate the positive.* While you may have plenty of bad news to communicate within your organization, remember that most people prefer to read positive messages instead of negative ones. And if they prefer a particular kind of message, that means chances are that they will read it and take it to heart. We understand that you'll sometimes need to report bad news, but when

you do so, always be sure to give your colleagues options for coun-
teracting the bad news.

THE TECHNOLOGY ADVANTAGE

As you've no doubt noticed, there has been a revolution in communications technology over the past decade or so. While communication
within and between organizations was once limited to telephone calls,
letters sent through the mail, and the occasional telegram or cable-
gram, today there is an amazing array of technology available for anyone who wants to use communications to his or her advantage. From fax
machines, to voice mail and e-mail, to mobile phones and pagers—and
much, much more—staying in touch with business associates is easier
and less expensive than ever.

And the *right* communications technology really can make a big
difference in the success of organizations, especially small businesses.
Why? Because small businesses are typically able to adopt and take
advantage of emerging communications technology more quickly than
can large businesses. Before committing to a major platform change
that could cost many thousands or even millions of dollars, large businesses understandably want to be sure that the platform is stable first.
This gives small businesses an opening that many of them are all too
happy to fill.

But, at the same time, the example of how small businesses are able
to leverage emerging communications technologies to their advantage
offers lessons that any organization can benefit from, including these:

- Emulate small businesses by implementing new technologies more
  rapidly and effectively than the competition.
- Create electronic links to other businesses.
- Use electronic bulletin boards and online data services to gain access to more market data and business opportunities, allowing your
  organization to quickly attack new opportunities.

- Use information links to form "virtual corporations" with other businesses, gaining increased market presence while enabling your organization to concentrate on what it does best.
- Take advantage of mobile computing, which can allow your company to compete around the world without setting up expensive branch offices.

Keep a close eye on fast-evolving communications technology. While not every item that hits the store shelves is going to be a winner, the right telecommunications technology implemented in the right way and in the right place can make your organization faster and more flexible and you more personally effective. The faster that information is distributed and acted on in your organization, the more competitive and successful your business will be.

─────────── **POP QUIZ!** ───────────

Effective communication is the lifeblood of any organization and every effective manager. Reflect on your ability to communicate and the contents of this chapter, then answer these questions:

1. What are the most important communication skills every manager needs?
2. What are advantages of effectively communicating with your employees?
3. Name two challenges and two opportunities of effective communication in organizations today.
4. Name several key aspects of any effective business communication, whether listening, speaking, or writing.
5. What are your communication strengths and weaknesses as a manager?

CHAPTER 12

Working with Teams

IT'S A NEW WORLD OUT THERE . . .

Teams and . . .

How they engage employees in their organizations.

How teams get things done.

Ensuring your teams are empowered.

Building an organization based on teamwork.

GETTING THINGS DONE WITH TEAMS

If you've been in any organization for more than 10 minutes, you've probably heard about the increasing importance of teams for making things happen. But, what's a team? And why should you bother? Couldn't you get what you need done all by yourself?

A team is two or more people who work together to achieve a common goal—say, creating a new product line, or bringing company policies up to date, or planning the company picnic. Teams work because they don't rely solely on the skills, knowledge, and abilities of just one person. By collecting and focusing the talent of a *group* of people—employees from different functions and levels of the organization—teams can solve even the most difficult problems. And because the front-line employees who are often tapped for teams are much closer to customers and vendors than are the men and women who manage them, the decisions they make are often better ones.

In this chapter, we'll consider why teams are more popular than ever; the different kinds of teams and how they work; the impact of empowered teams; and how technology is affecting the ways that teams get work done.

THE OLD WAYS ARE FADING FAST

In the good old days, most organizations were designed in a very simple fashion—as strict hierarchies, with the top managers or owners at the top, the middle managers and supervisors in the middle, and the workers at the bottom. This design—similar to the traditional military organization, where privates report to corporals, who report to sergeants, who report to captains, and so on, up to the commanding general—was reinforced both formally through organization charts and delegations of authority, and informally through such things as executive privileges, reserved parking spaces, executive washrooms, and the like.

While hierarchies have long been an effective way to run an organization, this is less so the case nowadays. In today's business-at-the-speed-of-light environment, organizations that are wedded to strict hierarchies—where orders have to travel through numerous levels of employees before they reach the workers who will implement them—cannot respond quickly enough to fast-changing market conditions. New forms of doing business—including the widespread use of teams, which can respond fast and flexibly—are taking hold, and the old ways of doing business are quickly going out of fashion.

So, why have the old ways of business given way to the new? There are a variety of reasons, which we will explore in the sections that follow.

The Impact of Downsizing

Interestingly enough, when times get tough for organizations and they are forced to cut costs and layoff employees, managers are often among the first to go. Why? Because, it can be argued, they don't really produce anything of value. Sure, they are responsible for creating budgets, and controlling costs, and writing procedures, and designing and organizing departments and procedures; very few managers actually produce products or deliver services to customers.

Some of you may recall the business-reengineering craze of the early 1990s when large corporations such as IBM, AT&T, General Motors, and others laid off hundreds of thousands of employees—all in the name of improving business efficiency and lowering costs. As it turns out, many of these people were managers who—top executives realized—would barely be missed when they were gone. As the supervisors and managers who filled the middle ranks of organizational hierarchies were disposed of, the hierarchies collapsed, leaving flat organizations with only a layer or two between top executives and frontline workers. Besides saving money, this outcome had the added benefit of breaking apart deep-seated, rigid hierarchies and leaving much faster and more flexible organizations in their wake.

While this was not a happy time for the people who lost their jobs (many of whom took early retirement, started their own businesses, or learned new job skills and found work elsewhere), this was a happy time for their newly trimmed down and responsive organizations. In fact, these retooled organizations saw improvements in a variety of different areas, including:

- *Decision making:* The decision-making process was a bad joke in many organizations—particularly large organizations—where bureaucracy, turf battles, and corporate politics reigned supreme. Decisions that should have taken minutes or hours at most instead took weeks or even months. But, as layers of middle managers were shown the door and hierarchies flattened, decisions were once again put on the fast track.
- *Communicating:* As layers of middle managers disappeared so did a lot of organizational friction, allowing communication to flow much more freely and much more quickly—from top to bottom and across departmental boundaries.
- *Responsiveness:* With fewer levels in the organization, employees can be empowered to be more responsive to customer needs as well as encouraged to take greater initiative in their jobs.

- *Bottom-line benefits:* Organizations that rid themselves of droves of middle managers—and their expensive pay and benefits packages—suddenly found themselves with a lot less cost and a lot more profit.
- *Movement of authority and power:*With the loss of many of their management and supervisory ranks, frontline employees were forced to take on more of the roles formerly reserved for management, including decision making, making hiring and firing decisions, drafting and controlling budgets, and much more. The result is that much authority and power in many organizations have migrated to where the action is—among their frontline employees.

- *Greater utilization of technology:* To keep current *and* connected, organizations are coming to rely more heavily on technology to better communicate and implement the organization's services.

Cooperation instead of Competition

While downsizing was a powerful force pushing many organizations away from the old model of strong hierarchy and toward the new model of teams, another force was also at work: an increasing desire for employees to work together—to cooperate—to achieve common goals rather than to compete against one another. The result is that organizations are no longer measuring employees only by their individual contributions but also by how effective they are as contributing members of their work teams.

To make organizational sense of this fundamental change, businesses are increasingly moving away from a structure of traditional, functional divisions that once separated organizational units (for example, manufacturing, sales, engineering, inventory, and so forth) from one another. In their place are *teams*—comprised of employees from different organizational units—whose members work together to perform tasks and achieve common goals. Most businesses still organize their operations by departments, divisions, and so forth, but smart managers now encourage, rather than discourage, their employees to cross formal organizational lines to get their work done more efficiently and effectively.

There are a number of benefits available to organizations that promote cooperation instead of competition among employees, including:

- *Reducing unproductive competition:* Competition is great when it's directed at your competitors, but when it's directed at employees against one another, then the results can be a detriment to employee harmony and the achievement of organizational goals—all of which work against the bottom line.

- *Sharing knowledge:* Employees who share knowledge quickly and widely are much more effective than employees who don't know what's going on. The most effective teams make a point to share knowledge and to reap the benefits thereof.
- *Fostering communication:* As we mentioned, an organization's formal structures—departments, divisions, and other organizational units—often act as walls to communication rather than facilitators of communication. By including members from a variety of different organizational units, teams can break down these walls, fostering communication in the process.
- *Achieving common goals:* Because the members of teams would rather win than lose, they are automatically motivated to work together to achieve common goals. And when managers reward employees for teamwork over individual performance, this motivation becomes that much stronger.

EMPOWERING YOUR TEAMS

The flattening of organizational structures that accompanied downsizing—along with the move toward cooperation and away from competition within organizations—has made employees more responsive to customer needs by encouraging the resolution of problems at the lowest possible level in the organization. This transfer of power, responsibility, and authority from higher level to lower level employees is what is commonly known as *empowerment*.

Although the term empowerment has become a bit cliché within most organizations, there is no getting around the fact that by empowering workers, managers place the responsibility for decision making with the employees who are in the best position to make the decision. The simple fact is that despite rumors to the contrary, few managers know everything about every aspect of their business, and they rely on their employees to obtain this knowledge and then use it to get things

> **(?) ASK BOB AND PETER:** I have been asked to determine the temperament within our team of approximately 140 people and to then make recommendations for required improvements. We are planning to issue a survey to all staff to determine the current state of morale; we will then benchmark our staff and measure again in six months. Can you suggest survey questions to help us obtain this information in an accurate way?
>
> We have a couple of suggestions for you. First, make sure that the answers are completely confidential. Make sure that employees have no fear of retribution for "telling it like it is." Second, your questions should get to the heart of the matter as directly as possible. Ask employees to rate their own morale and then the morale of their group on a scale of 0 to 10. Ask them to name the top five morale problems in the organization and the top five things that have improved morale in the organization. Ask them to tell you exactly what they would change about the organization to improve morale. Also ask them what they would keep. The point here is to get specific information—not vague, mushy responses. Finally, when you pinpoint morale problems, do something to really solve them. If you don't, you're going to create another morale problem!

done. By trusting employees to do the job that needs to be done—and getting out of their way—employee creativity and initiative will be unlocked, leading to immediate benefits to the organization's bottom line.

TEAMS WORK

Why do teams work? Teams work because they involve the right people (those closest to customers, problems, and opportunities) in making decisions that are most important to their organizations. And because they include the right people, when they are given appropriate authority as well, they can make these decisions much more quickly and flexibly than can the rigid hierarchies of old.

Smaller and Nimbler

The fast-increasing rate and scope of change in the global business environment puts a premium on organizational structures that can respond quickly to change. By breaking down into smaller organizational units such as teams—and giving them real decision-making power—even the largest companies can become nimbler than their competitors.

Customers want to get their products and services faster than ever before, but they also expect lower prices. Because of their ability to better respond to opportunities and to facilitate decision making, teams are an essential element in allowing organizations to deliver products and services "any time, any place" and at prices that meet—and even exceed—the customer expectations.

Innovative and Adaptable

By unlocking the creativity, knowledge, and talent of all employees, teams can lead to increased innovation. And because they are smaller and nimbler, teams can also more easily adapt to changes in their external environments. Both Xerox Corporation and Hewlett-Packard have found that by intertwining design, engineering, and manufacturing functions in the development of new products, they are able to dramatically speed up the process of taking a new product from concept to production.

And while teams used to be considered useful only for projects of short duration (say, organizing that company picnic), there is an increasing realization that teams can also be effective for long-term projects and for enhancing the way that organizations do business over long periods of time. The result is permanent teams that are built into organizational structures rather than just shoehorned in, making them that much more powerful and effective.

CREATING A TEAM CULTURE

Once you decide to create a team to address some organizational opportunity or problem, you're faced with a decision: What kind of team
should you set up? There are three major categories of teams, including: *formal, informal,* and *self-managed.* You probably won't be surprised to find out that each offers its own set of advantages and
disadvantages which we will explore in the sections that follow.

Formal Teams

A *formal team* is a team that is chartered by an organization's management and tasked to address specific issues or to achieve specific goals.
These issues and goals can be anything of importance to the business—
from determining whether to move production offshore, to addressing
how to capitalize on changing customer preferences, to planning an annual employee awards program. Types of formal teams include:

- *Task forces:* These are formal teams assembled on a temporary
  basis to address specific problems or issues. A task force could, for
  example, be created by management to get to the bottom of recent
  customer complaints about product quality. Task forces most often
  are given deadlines for addressing their problems or issues and reporting their findings back to management.
- *Committees:* Committees are long-term or permanent teams designed to perform an ongoing, specific organizational task. Examples include safety committees required by company liability
  insurance policies and employee morale committees designed to
  make the workplace more fun for workers. While committees
  themselves may exist unchanged for many years, their membership
  most often undergoes constant change as members are appointed
  and relieved of their duties.
- *Command teams:* Command teams combine some aspects of a regular hierarchy with teams because they are comprised of a manager

---

THE REAL WORLD

Working with teams is a critical skill in any organization. Teams help you to integrate a variety of skills and perspectives, but not without its challenges. It is easy to find fault with a team or individuals who are part of it. Your energy is better served to look for opportunities to *build* the team and reinforce the team's progress and results. The best managers come to value and respect diversity of opinion and those employees who challenge their thinking because they know it will lead to better decisions that are easier to implement. Keep this in mind as you select teams and avoid the tendency to have team members who think and act just like yourself. Remember the maxim about groups: "None of us is better than all of us."

---

or supervisor and all the employees who report directly to him or her. While employee input and suggestions are often solicited, there is no question that the manager or supervisor is in charge and that he or she will ultimately make important team decisions. Some common examples of command teams include disaster operations teams, company sales teams, and management teams.

As integral parts of the official structures of the organization in which they function, formal teams play an important role, both in facilitating communications between the different levels of the organization, and in organizing people to get things done. And although other types of teams are becoming more popular in organizations, there will always be a place for formal teams in the overall scheme of things.

Informal Teams

Casual associations of employees that spontaneously develop within an organization's formal structure are known as *informal teams* and some observers consider them to be more important in how work gets done than their formal team siblings. Informal teams can form and disband anytime, anyplace, and they may arise for a wide variety of reasons. An organization might, for example, have an informal team of employees who like to play softball after work, or who have banded together to address problems with indoor air pollution at a manufacturing facility, or who have decided to organize a company trip to Las Vegas.

Informal teams are important to organizations for the following reasons:

- They foster communication among employees in different parts and at different levels of the organization. Because informal teams are not chartered by management, they are safe for employees to speak freely and without fear of negative repercussions.
- They provide a way for employees who might not usually be tapped by management to lead formal teams to practice leadership roles. While the mailroom clerk might not, for example, be management's leading candidate to lead the site selection committee for a new factory, he might very well make a bang-up captain of the company bowling team.

Sometimes it's best to limit team membership only to people who are going to be most likely to help solve a problem. That's the idea behind *ad hoc teams*. If, for example, there's a problem with the company's computer network, it makes a lot more sense to create an ad hoc team comprised of information technology (IT) employees than to include employees whose job it is to cook lunch in the company cafeteria.

Self-Managed Teams

The new kid on the team block, *self-managed teams* hold much promise for organizations by combining the best attributes of both formal and informal teams. While self-managed teams are most often created by a manager, when given sufficient authority and autonomy, they quickly take on many of the roles that would normally be served by the organization's managers including making decisions, hiring and firing employees, creating and managing budgets, and much more. Other names for self-managed teams include *high-performance teams, cross-functional teams,* or *superteams.*

The most effective self-managing teams are:

- Made up of people from different parts of the organization.
- Small because large groups create communication problems.
- Self-managing and empowered to act because referring decisions back up the line wastes time and often leads to poorer decisions.
- Multifunctional because that's the best—if not the only—way to keep the actual product and its essential delivery system clearly visible and foremost in everyone's mind.

It's a difficult thing for managers to give up their authority to a team of employees, but self-managed teams are becoming more common in today's business world. As they prove their worth, the question is less "Is there a self-managed team in your future," but "How soon will you become a member of a self-managed team?"

Empowered Teams

Despite all the talk about collaborative leadership, participative management, and self-managing team, real employee empowerment is still rare. How can you tell when a team is truly empowered, and when it's not? Here are some tell-tale characteristics of empowered, self-managing teams:

- They make the team's important decisions.
- They interview and select their leaders.

- They invite new team members (and remove members who aren't working out).
- They set their own goals and make their own commitments.
- They design and perform much of their own training.
- They distribute and receive rewards as a team.

Unfortunately, this ideal of empowered, self-managed teams is often quite different from the reality. Many employees—members of so-called self-managed teams—report that while they have a greater voice in the team process, key decisions are still being made by their organization's top managers. This fact again points out that it is often difficult for managers (whose job, after all, is to manage) to give up their own authority and to hand it over to teams of employees, regardless of how skilled or insightful they may be.

If teams in your organization are not truly empowered, there are a number of things you can do to alter the status quo, starting with this list of suggested actions:

- *Make your teams empowered, not merely participative:* Don't just invite employees to participate in teams, grant team members the real authority and power that they need to make independent decisions.

    —Allow your teams to make long-range and strategic decisions, not just cosmetic or procedural ones.

    —Permit the team to choose its own team leaders; don't appoint them for the team.

    —Allow the team to determine its goals and commitments; don't assign them yourself.

    —Make sure that all team members have influence by involving them in the decision-making process, and then do everything possible to honor the decisions the team makes.

- *Remove the source of conflicts:* Managers are often unwilling to live with the decisions made by empowered teams. Be willing to grant teams autonomy and authority, and then be ready to live with the decisions that these empowered teams make.

—Recognize and work out personality conflicts.

—Fight turfism and middle-management resistance when and wherever it is encountered.

—Work hard to unify manager and team member views.

—Do what you can to minimize the stress on team members of downsizing and process improvement tasks.

- *Change other significant factors that influence team effectiveness:* Other factors can indicate that an organization has not yet brought true empowerment to its employees. Redouble your efforts to bring empowerment about by:

  —Allowing your teams to discipline poorly performing members themselves and without your influence or intervention.

  —Minimizing the impact of peer pressure in attaining high team performance.

  —Making a point to provide team members with the same kinds of skills training as is provided to supervisors and managers in your organization.

Empowered teams don't just happen all by themselves. To come about, supervisors and managers must make concerted and ongoing efforts to pass authority and autonomy from themselves to teams in their organizations. Until they do, then no team can be truly empowered or self-managing.

TEAMS AND TECHNOLOGY

There are three dominant forces shaping twenty-first century organizations:

1. A high-involvement workplace with self-managed teams and other devices for empowering employees.

2. A new emphasis on managing business processes rather than functional departments.

3. The evolution of information technology to the point where knowledge, accountability, and results can be distributed rapidly anywhere in the organization.

In each of these three forces, communication and information technology plays key roles. The effective design, management, and implementation of new technologies are therefore a critical factor in the competitiveness and long-term success of today's organizations.

Information, however, is notoriously difficult to manage. According to Peter Drucker in *Management: Tasks, Responsibilities, Practices* (New York: Harper & Row, 1974): "Information activities present a special organizational problem. Unlike most other result-producing activities, they are not concerned with one stage of the process but with the entire process itself. This means that they have to be both centralized and decentralized."

The better and more effective use of information technology enables organizations to rely more on teams to make decisions and less on individual supervisors and managers—leading to reductions in the numbers of supervisors and managers required to staff specific departments and functions. These reductions often lead to dramatic cost savings which flow directly to the company's bottom line.

For those managers who remain, new skills are required to become coaches, supporters, and facilitators of self-managing teams of front-line employees. Instead of trying to control the organization, managers and supervisors find themselves in a new job: to inspire workers instead of commanding them. By doing so, they can have a major impact on the effectiveness and long-term success of their organizations, while encouraging employees at all levels of the organization to grow and to mature in their new roles as team leaders and decision makers.

POP QUIZ!

Being a manager today requires more than a casual acquaintance with human behavior and how to create an environment that will encourage and allow your employees to give their very best at all times. Reflect for a few moments on what you have learned in this chapter; then ask yourself the following questions:

1. To what extent do you rely on teams to get things done in your organization?

2. Are team members in your organization committed? If not, why not? What could be done to improve teams and effective teamwork?

3. What are your strengths in working with and being a part of a team? What are your weaknesses?

4. In what ways do you empower teams, giving them the authority and autonomy they need to get their jobs done? What more could you do?

5. How do you track the results of teams in your organization and hold them accountable for their results?

CHAPTER 13

Making Meetings More Effective

IT'S A NEW WORLD OUT THERE . . .

Meetings and . . .

How they enable teams to get work done.

Getting the most out of meetings.

Understanding common meeting problems—and their fixes.

Improving your meetings.

MEETINGS PUT TEAMS TO WORK

Meetings are the primary forum in which groups conduct business and communicate with one another. With the proliferation of teams in business today, it pays to master the basic skills of meeting management.

Teams are clearly an idea whose time has come. As organizations continue to flatten their hierarchies and empower front-line workers with more responsibility and authority, teams are the visible and often inevitable result. Consider how one of the best companies runs meetings to respond to this new, team-oriented business environment.

- Say what you will about Jack Welch, former chairman of General Electric (GE), he is one of the most effective and successful managers in the history of American business. Part of his success was a direct result of moving his company away from the old-style autocratic leadership model and toward a new model of participative management based on teams. This new leadership model required a new model of meetings, called *work out* meetings, which bring workers and managers together in open forums where workers are allowed to ask any question they want and managers are required to respond.

- The results of Welch's influence can be observed at GE's Bayamón, Puerto Rico, lightning arrester plant, where employees have been organized into self-managing, cross-functional teams that are responsible for specific plant functions—shipping, assembly, and so forth—comprising employees from all parts of the plant. As a result, when a team discusses changes that need to be made in their operations, employees from throughout the organization will be a part of the discussion and decision-making process, tearing down the organizational silos that often get in the way of communication. In addition, hourly workers run the meetings on their own, while *advisors*—GE's term for salaried employees—participate only at the team's request.

While considered an experiment, Bayamón produced clear and convincing evidence that GE's approach was quite successful. A year after startup, the plant's employees measured 20 percent higher in productivity than their closest counterpart in the mainland United States. Not only that, but management projected a further 20 percent increase in the following year.

Unfortunately, meetings in many organizations are at best a waste of time and at worst a severe detriment to efficiency and effectiveness. Poorly run meetings are routine; instead of contributing to an organization's efficiency and effectiveness, most meetings make employees less efficient and less effective. When was the last time that you actually looked forward to participating in a meeting rather than trying to figure out some way to get out of it? But, let us make it as clear and unambiguous as we can: Every minute counts; it's your job to ensure that the meetings you attend have value for the organization.

WHAT'S WRONG WITH MEETINGS?

What does your gut tell you about meetings in your organization? If your organization is like most organizations, the majority of meetings are a waste of time. Meeting experts have determined that approximately 53 percent of all the time spent in meetings is unproductive, worthless, and of little consequence. While this is bad news in itself, when you consider that most businesspeople spend at least 25 percent of their working hours in meetings, with upper management spending more than double that time in meetings, you can see that bad meetings are a real recipe for organizational disaster.

But why do so many meetings go so wrong, and is there something you can do to fix them within your organization? In our book *Better*

ASK BOB AND PETER: Do you know of any good training programs to help employees improve their public speaking skills?

Although there are a variety of programs available to help employees with their public speaking skills, you might consider the following: (1) Communispond is a business that specializes in preparing employees for speaking publicly and before one another. Bob once took a three-day class with Communispond and was impressed with its quality and effectiveness. Find them on the Web at www.communispond.com. (2) Joining Toastmasters International is a terrific and inexpensive way to learn how to become a better and more effective public speaker. The environment is low pressure and supportive, and chapters meet often—usually once a week. Check them out at www.toastmasters.org. (3) Many community colleges offer classes in public speaking. Contact one near you to find out what's available.

Business Meetings (New York: McGraw-Hill, 1994), we discuss a few of the reasons:

- *Too many meetings take place.* It seems like someone in every organization is having a meeting almost every day for some reason or another, whether the topic of the meeting is important enough to merit it. The result? A lot of time spent in meetings and not so much time getting actual work done. It's no surprise that many people find themselves thinking (often out loud), "How am I supposed to get any work done with all these meetings?"
- *The meeting starts late.* The tendency is to wait for those people who are late, especially if that includes your boss or someone of higher rank in the organization. Unfortunately, this wastes the time of all those who are waiting, essentially punishing them for being on time and rewarding those who were late, making it even easier for them (and others) to be late the next time as well.

Ask Bob and Peter: How different is it managing a business on the Internet compared to a regular business? Whereas the office provides a physical meeting place, an Internet business is widespread with no physical meeting place.

You've noticed one of the most interesting nuances of managing people (i.e., in an office) versus managing them remotely (i.e., via the Internet). In a regular office environment, managers interact with their employees all the time. They sit in meetings with them, visit with them, talk with them in the hallway, listen to their stories of success—and failure—and, as a result, they often develop very strong working relationships with them. Unfortunately, when you manage remotely (through the Internet) you may go months without having time to form strong interpersonal bonds with your employees. And while you can certainly work with and manage employees via e-mail, phone calls, faxes, and the like, it's not the same as being in the same room with them. The solution to this is to be sure that time and money are set aside for the employees of the organization to meet with their managers and coworkers on a periodic basis, typically a minimum of once every two weeks. These meetings should focus on giving managers and employees the opportunity to meet one another and participate in team-building exercises that require them to work together to achieve certain goals. You might, for example, have a monthly marketing strategy meeting or a quarterly business planning meeting. The choice depends on what kind of meeting meets your needs and the needs of your organization. By creating opportunities for managers and employees to work together to achieve common goals, developing strong interpersonal bonds and relationships, whether the business is run over the Internet or not, you will help employees achieve their goals and, thus, the goals of the organization.

- *The meeting has no focus.* Does every meeting you attend have an agenda and a clear plan for getting from the beginning to the end? If you answered "yes," then we would be very surprised indeed. Most often, meetings are a proliferation of personal agendas, digressions, diversions, off-topic tangents, and worse. These results all serve to throw meetings out of focus, off track, and into the annals of countless other worthless wastes of time.

- *Attendees are unprepared.* Often individuals come unprepared and may not even know why they've been invited to attend. This means that precious time is wasted either bringing all the attendees up to speed on the issues, or attendees simply mentally check out of the meeting, imagining all the things they could be doing with the time they are wasting in the meeting!

- *Certain individuals dominate the proceedings.* It seems that there's always someone in a meeting (in large meetings, more than one person) who decides to be the star of the show and to make his or her points as loudly and as often as possible. Aside from their obnoxious behavior, the problem is that these individuals often intimidate the other participants and stifle their contributions—not the outcome you need to accomplish the goals of the meeting.

- *The meeting lasts too long.* Rather than let the participants leave after the business at hand is completed, most meeting leaders allow meetings to expand to fill the time allotted to them. The result is that meetings often drag on and on and on—well past the time when they have stopped being productive.

THE EIGHT KEYS TO GREAT MEETINGS

Although many meetings are a big waste of time, they don't have to be. The cure is readily available and inexpensive and can be easy to implement. Here's what we've found to be the most useful advice for having more effective meetings:

THE REAL WORLD

As Peter Drucker once observed: "One can work or meet, but not both" (from *The Effective Executive*, New York: HarperCollins, 1993). No one seems to like meetings, but they seem to be a necessary evil of organizational life that is here to stay. To get the most out of the meetings you are a part of, play an active role. If the group is bogged down, for example, don't be passive and start doodling or daydreaming, speak up! Summarize where things seem to be and make a suggestion for progressing, for example, "It seems as though all the opinions on the issue have been raised, so should we take a vote to decide the issue?" or "Sally, I think John is agreeing with most of what you said, but simply wants to clarify how we can avoid this situation in the future." Speaking up to say what others are thinking but not saying will show leadership in the group and, in most cases, be a welcomed intervention. And if the group has finished discussing the issues you were present for, ask if anyone minds if you are dismissed to deal with more pressing work at your desk. Respecting the group and its time starts with respecting yourself and your time.

1. *Be prepared.* It takes only a little time to prepare for a meeting, and the payoff is well worth it—significantly increased meeting effectiveness. This should include an initial chairperson's orientation speech in which you summarize the reason the group is meeting and the desired decisions or actions that will result.

2. *Have an agenda.* An agenda—the plan for your meeting—is essential. Don't even think about winging a meeting without it. Even better, distribute the agenda to participants before the meeting. This way, meeting participants can be prepared for the meeting in advance, and you'll multiply its effectiveness many times over.

3. *Start on time and end on time.* Every meeting should have established start and end times. Be sure to start your meetings at the appointed time, and run no longer than the established end time. Sure, you can occasionally make exceptions to the end rule when meeting participants agree to extend the meeting, but you'll start losing participant effectiveness as they begin to worry about other commitments.

4. *Have fewer but better meetings.* Makes sense, doesn't it? Schedule meetings only when they are absolutely necessary. At all costs, avoid standing meetings such as, "We'll meet every Tuesday at 2 P.M.," which encourages meeting for meeting's sake, instead of with a clear sense of purpose. And when you call a meeting, make sure that it has an agenda and that you do whatever you can to keep it on track and effective. And if the reason for calling a meeting is resolved prior to the start time, cancel it. Everyone will be impressed and grateful that you did.

5. *Think inclusion, not exclusion.* Don't just invite anyone and everyone to your meetings—select only those participants necessary to get the job done. Likewise, don't exclude people who need to be present for the matters being discussed. Then make sure all who are invited know why and what is expected of them when they attend. This helps them each to prepare and to bring the appropriate information with them.

6. *Maintain focus.* Stay on topic at all times and avoid the temptation to get off track or to follow interesting (but unproductive) digressions that take you no closer to solving the issues that were the reason for meeting in the first place. Digressions and off-topic discussions might be entertaining, but they are a waste of time for everyone involved. Stick to the topic and the timelines you set for each item on the agenda. Vary from that only with the permission and agreement of the group.

7. *Capture action items.* Have a system for capturing, summarizing, and assigning action items to individual team members, which can

often be handled by assigning roles to attendees such as scribe, timekeeper, and summarizer. And be sure to follow up team member progress on assigned action items to ensure that they get done.

8. *Get feedback.* Remember: Feedback is the breakfast of champions. Feedback tells you not only what you did right but also what you did wrong—providing you with strong ideas on how to make your future meetings more effective. Request meeting participants to give you their candid feedback—verbally or in writing—and then be sure to use it. The more suggestions you implement, the more you'll get from your employees.

───────────────── **POP QUIZ!** ─────────────────

Meetings are one of the key tools for teams to get work done in their organizations. Reflect for a few moments on what you have learned in this chapter; then ask yourself the following questions:

1. In what ways do your employees find meetings useful in your organization?
2. What do you do to prepare for meetings? What do you expect from others?
3. How do you communicate your expectations to meeting participants?
4. How do you ensure that meetings achieve the intended goals?
5. Do you have too many meetings, too few, or just enough? How could you improve?

PART

V

Management Challenges

CHAPTER 14

Discipline and Corrective Action

IT'S A NEW WORLD OUT THERE . . .

Discipline and . . .

How it helps managers correct employee performance.

Discipline isn't a dirty word.

Focusing on employee performance instead of personalities.

Dealing with performance issues versus misconduct.

How to discipline employees.

Looking to the future.

WHY DISCIPLINE?

Every manager dreams of a workplace where every employee does the job he or she was hired to do and does it well. Of course, in the real world, your employees will make mistakes, and some will sometimes exhibit poor attitudes. While everyone makes the occasional mistake, when your employees make repeated, serious mistakes, when they fail to meet their performance goals and standards, or when it seems that they'd rather be working anywhere but where they are, you will need to discipline your employees. Why?

First, employees who aren't doing the job cost your organization more than do the employees who are. Poor performance and poor attitudes directly and negatively impact your work unit's ability to be efficient and effective.

Second, if other employees see that you're letting their coworkers get away with poor performance, they will often follow suit, decreasing the morale and performance of your entire work unit as a result.

In this chapter, we explore the importance of dealing with employee performance issues before they become major problems that can impact your entire organization. We'll find out why it's important to focus on performance and not personality and discover how implementing a consistent system of discipline can work for you.

WHAT DOES DISCIPLINE MEAN TO YOU?

What does discipline mean to you? What does discipline mean in your organization? Is discipline a positive experience in your organization, or are employees always on pins and needles, afraid that they may be the next one to feel your wrath?

THE BIG PICTURE

JOHN THOMSON
Chairman, Thomson Industries, Inc.

Question: Are there times when patience can make a big difference in a challenging situation?

Answer: Definitely. One time we decided to acquire a product group from one of the largest manufacturers in the world—General Motors (GM). We had heard rumors that they were going to try to spin it off, and I always said that we should be in that business. Finally, our president came to me and said, "I'm getting nowhere; what do I do?" And I said, "Well, I would write to the chairman of General Motors and ask him if this is in fact true." And he said, "Well, I'll never hear from him." So we wrote to him, and someone further down the ladder responded to us. Eight months later we got a call from a large New York investment banking firm saying that the product group was going to be spun off by GM and asking if we were interested in a package. We got a packet and found out that we were one of about 100 respondents that had expressed interest in buying this group—from *Fortune* 10 companies to small, private entities. It took close to 10 months to negotiate the contract and negotiate the deal, but we knew we weren't going to win in a bidding war. But we tried to put our team together and have the patience to work with GM, which was quite frustrating. And we waited and waited and competitors dropped out or were eliminated by GM or by Solomon and, at the end of the day, we ended up winning the right to purchase this particular product group from GM. Right down through the last week, a *Fortune* 10 company tried to pressure GM into selling to them. And GM said no—that we were the right fit. And they were obviously trying to buy it by intriguing them with more cash. So the patience paid off.

Question: How does growth impact your team?

Answer: I'm proud of how the company's grown, and we are becoming a global company. We have operations now in Singapore and Malaysia and England. One of the things I'm particularly proud of was a real team effort. It spawned out of the acquisition of the products group from General Motors. Our team was able to figure out and put together a concept that no one else was able to develop and bring a product that was priced way out of limits down to where it was a viable contract for General Motors. What started out to be a three-year contract has run 10 years now, making actuators for their antilock braking system. And out of that, we became a supplier of the year for General Motors for three consecutive years so far. General Motors has 30,000 suppliers, roughly, and they choose approximately 150 per year out of the 30,000 on which to bestow this honor. We are one of the 30 that have won it three times in a row out of 30,000 suppliers. That was a total team effort from start to finish, from inception through winning the award.

Believe it or not, employee discipline can be a positive experience. When you've got a problem with an employee who is not responding to gentle coaching or direction, discipline is guaranteed to get your employees' attention. The primary goal of discipline isn't to punish your employees; it is to help guide them back to a satisfactory job performance. Sometimes this step isn't possible, and you have no choice but to terminate employees who can't perform satisfactorily (more on this in Chapter 15, "Terminating Employees").

Although there are many different reasons to discipline your employees, these reasons fall into one of two broad categories:

1. *Performance problems:* Employees have goals and standards that they must meet as a part of their jobs. For a purchasing agent, a standard may be to process at least 25 requisitions a day. For a production manager, a goal may be to decrease manufacturing costs by 10 percent. When employees fail to meet their performance goals, discipline is required.

2. *Misconduct:* Sometimes employees break the rules and must be disciplined. An employee who steals office supplies and takes them home, for example, should be disciplined and—in the case of continued abuse—terminated.

The term *discipline* covers a range of possible outcomes, from simple verbal counseling to termination. Which outcome you apply as a manager depends on the nature of the problem, its severity, and the work history of the employee involved. If the problem is an isolated incident and the employee normally performs well, the discipline will be less severe than if the problem is repeated and persistent.

Discipline should always be carried out as soon after the incident as possible—employees will better relate the discipline to their actions when this is the case and your message will be much stronger and relevant. When too much time passes between an incident and the discipline, your employee may forget the specifics of the incident—losing the impact of your message. In addition, you send the message that the problem isn't that serious because you didn't bother doing anything about it for so long.

Practice effective discipline by noticing performance shortcomings or misconduct when they are minor *before* these problems become serious. Managers who don't discipline their employees are part of the problem, not the solution, because through their lassitude they allow poor performance or acts of misconduct to escalate. It's your job as a manager to support and guide your employees and to let them know what's expected of them.

Don't put off discipline until tomorrow, and especially don't look the other way and hope that your employees' bad behavior disappears. Chances are, it won't. By looking in the other direction and ignoring the negative behavior, you're doing a disservice to the employees who need your guidance, to the employees who are working at or above standard, and to your organization.

PERFORMANCE IS THE FOCUS

You're not a psychiatrist, you're a manager. Your job isn't to analyze your workers' personalities or to try to figure out why your employees act the way they do, so don't even try. Your job is to compare your employees' performance against the standards that you and your employees agree to and to take action when the two diverge by rewarding them for performing above standard, or disciplining them for performing below standard.

Discipline and compassion are not mutually exclusive; you can and should take family problems, financial difficulties, or other non-job-related pressures into account when you discipline employees. You can give your employees the opportunity to get through their difficulties—by suggesting some time off or a temporary reassignment of duties—but they eventually will have to return to meeting their performance standards.

For discipline to work, its application must be consistent and fair. Rushing to judgment before you have a chance to get all the facts is a mistake—especially in complex situations where uncovering the facts may take some time. Know the facts before you discipline and act impartially and without favoritism. This means that if one employee does something wrong, you can't ignore the same behavior in your other employees. Not only do you risk the loss of employee respect, but you're leaving yourself open to charges of favoritism and perhaps even discrimination and bias.

Remember, your employees are ultimately responsible for their performance and their behavior. You can't, and shouldn't, cover for their

ASK BOB AND PETER: My staff constantly quarrel and act jealous among themselves. It creates a situation where I am unable to make them operate like a team. Do I go for individual or group counsel? Any better advice?

Hmmm . . . there are a few things for you to consider as you try to sort out this problem. For one, exactly why is there so much quarreling and jealousy? Meet with each of your employees—one-on-one—and talk about it. Are the causes personal in nature, or are they created by the work environment? For example, some employees may believe that you are favoring certain employees over others, or morale may be low because of low pay, long hours, and the like. They might be competing for your attention. Or maybe they just don't like one another. In any case, the first step is to get to the root of the problems and identify them so you can determine what changes need to be made. Next, you need to remove the sources of conflict within your organization. For example, if certain employees are being favored over others, you have to remove that source of conflict by giving everyone an equal shot at your time and at the rewards of your organization, whatever they may be. Finally, build teamwork within your staff. To do this, you need to incentivize team behavior by rewarding your employees whenever they act the way you want them to. You can do this via verbal or written praise (preferably delivered in front of the other staff members) or by giving them more tangible rewards such as movie passes, gift certificates, time off, or whatever items they respond to. You should also run your staff through some teamwork training. There are many exercises available that can help your employees learn how to work together as a team and to see the benefits of doing so. Check with your human resources or training department for assistance. If your organization doesn't have these departments, check your local bookstore for books on the topic of building teams.

mistakes and misdeeds and you shouldn't do their work for them. Ongoing patterns of substandard performance or misconduct must be dealt with, not ignored.

THE TWO TRACKS OF DISCIPLINE

There are two key reasons for disciplining employees: performance problems and misconduct. The two-track system of discipline devotes a complete track—a unified set of actions—to each one of these reasons. The two-track system assumes that misconduct is a much more serious transgression than a performance issue. While misconduct is the result of a willful act, performance problems are not necessarily the direct fault of the employee and can often be easily corrected with proper training or motivation.

We are big believers in the concept of *progressive discipline*—selecting the least severe disciplinary action that results in the behavior that you want If, for example, your employee responds to coaching or verbal counseling in the case of a minor disciplinary problem, then it would be major overkill (not to mention punitive and counterproductive) to give him a written warning or suspension.

The first step in conducting discipline using the two-step system is to decide whether you're trying to correct performance-related behaviors or misconduct. The next step is to determine the least severe disciplinary action that will correct the negative behavior. A minor transgression may require only to conduct a verbal counseling, for example, but a more major transgression may require you to suspend your employee without pay for a week.

Your organization's system for disciplining employees may differ from the one that we outline in this chapter—perhaps significantly. If you're dealing with union-represented employees, for example, you're going to be required to work within the system proscribed by the contract between the union and your firm. Be sure to review your organization's policies and labor relations practices and procedures before you discipline your employees.

Dealing with Performance Problems: The First Track

Every one of your employees should have a job description and a set of performance standards. These documents will be the basis for disciplining your employees, so make sure first of all that they are available, and that they are well done and complete.

Employee performance can generally be placed into one of three broad categories:

1. Outstanding performance.
2. Acceptable performance.
3. Unacceptable performance.

When it comes to employee discipline, you're primarily concerned with correcting unacceptable performance. You generally won't be disciplining your employees for performing at an outstanding or acceptable level. Your first concern is to identify employees who aren't working up to standard and to correct their performance.

The following discipline steps are listed in order of least to most severe. Use the least severe step that results in the behavior you want. If that step doesn't do the trick, move down the list to the next step:

1. *Verbal counseling:* This form of discipline is the most common and the least severe, and most managers take this step first when they want to correct an employee's performance. Verbal counseling can range from a simple, spontaneous correction performed in the hallway to a more formal, sit-down meeting in your office. *Note:* You usually don't document verbal counseling in your employees' files.

2. *Written counseling:* When verbal counseling doesn't have the desired effect on performance or when the magnitude of performance problems warrants its use, written counseling should be applied. Written counseling takes the counseling process one step further by documenting your employees' performance shortcomings in the form of a written document, most often a memo. Written counseling is presented to employees in one-on-one sessions in the supervisor's office and, after the employee has an opportunity to read the document, verbal discussions regarding the employee's plans to improve his or her performance ensue. This documentation is placed in the employee's personnel file.

3. *Negative performance evaluation:* If verbal and written counseling fail to improve your employee's performance, a negative performance evaluation will ensue. Because performance evaluations are generally given only annually, if at all, they're not usually very useful for dealing with acute situations. However, if verbal and written counseling is not having the impact you seek, negative performance evaluations are a good next step.

4. *Termination:* Termination is the ultimate form of discipline for employees who are performing unsatisfactorily, and it is your best—and only—option when all other measures fail. Terminating employees is not fun; consider it as an option only after you exhaust all other avenues. In these days of wrongful termination lawsuits and multimillion-dollar judgments, you must document employees' performance shortcomings very well and support them with the facts before you terminate an employee, not after.

Dealing with Misconduct: The Second Track

Misconduct is an entirely different issue from performance problems, so it has its own discipline track. Misconduct is generally considered a much more serious offense than performance shortcomings because it indicates a fundamental problem with your employees' attitudes or ethical beliefs.

The discipline that results from misconduct has more immediate consequences to your employees than does the discipline that results from performance problems. Improving performance may take time—weeks or even months—but when you discipline your employees for misconduct, you put them on notice that their behavior won't be tolerated. Failure to immediately cure the misconduct can lead quickly to suspension and termination.

The following discipline steps in this second track are listed from least severe to most severe. The particular level of discipline you'll select depends on the severity of the misconduct and the employee's work record:

1. *Verbal warning:* If the misconduct is minor or if this is a first offense, the verbal warning provides the least severe option for putting your employees on notice that their behavior won't be tolerated. In many cases of misconduct, a verbal warning will be all you need to turn around your employee's behavior.

2. *Written warning:* Not every employee will get the message when you give them a verbal warning, so you may need to move up to the written warning. Written warnings are considered to be more serious than a verbal warning because the warning is documented in your employees' personnel files. Written warnings are performed by an employee's immediate supervisor.

3. *Reprimand:* Repeated or serious misconduct results in a reprimand, which is generally performed in much the same way as a written warning. The difference is that a manager higher up in the organization gives the reprimand instead of the employee's immediate supervisor. The reprimand makes clear that it is the employee's last chance to correct his or her behavior before suspension or termination.

> **?** **Ask Bob and Peter:** I was recently transferred back to the store that I managed for four years. Since I came back, there is a new employee who is pulling our team apart. I have tried different approaches to turn her around including being her buddy, training her more—which just gets her angry—and being strict with her. She has become lazy, and she has no focus; how can I motivate her to improve her performance?
>
> Business is built on relationships, and when relationships become tangled, your business can suffer. However, instead of focusing on the personality issues among your employees, focus on their performance. Do your employees have clear goals, and are you measuring their progress toward meeting these goals? If not, you'll see a huge difference once you start doing so. By the way, we think it's always a good idea to ask employees for their opinions—don't confuse being new with not having good ideas. New employees—unfettered by years of corporate conditioning—can often come up with the very best ideas.

4. *Suspension:* A *suspension,* or mandatory leave without pay, is used when other, less severe attempts at employee discipline fail to cure serious or repeated misconduct. Employees are also given nondisciplinary suspensions while they're being investigated on charges of misconduct, although employees are usually paid while the manager or other company official reviews the case.

5. *Termination:* When employee misconduct is extreme or repeated, then termination may be your best choice in disciplining a worker. Termination is usually the immediate option for extreme violations of safety rules, theft, gross insubordination, and other serious misconduct. See Chapter 15 for more information about terminating employees.

THE FIVE STEPS OF DISCIPLINE

There are five steps that should always form the basis of your discipline script. Follow these steps and you can be sure that your employees will clearly understand what the problem is and what they need to do to correct it.

Step 1: Describe the Unacceptable Behavior

Exactly what is your employee doing that is unacceptable? Be specific in your description, and don't use vague statements such as, "You've got a bad attitude," "You're not performing as well as your coworkers," or "Your work habits need improvement."

When you discipline employees, their unacceptable behaviors must be related directly to specific performance standards that have not been met or to specific policies that have been broken. Specify exactly what the employee did wrong and when the behavior occurred, and be sure to focus your attention on the behavior and not on the individual.

Here are some examples:

- "You produced only 25 service reports last month instead of the required standard of 40 per month."
- "You failed the drug test that you took on Friday."
- "You have been late to work every day this week."

Step 2: Express the Impact to the Work Unit

An employee's poor performance or misconduct doesn't just negatively impact him or her, it also has a negative impact on the work unit and the organization as a whole. When an employee underperforms, for example, another employee may have to be assigned to pick up the work that isn't getting done. This takes the other employee away from the work that he or she should be doing, ultimately having a negative impact on the organization's bottom line.

Continuing with the examples that we started in the preceding section, here are the next steps in your discipline script:

- "Because of your below-standard performance, the work unit didn't meet its overall targets for the month."
- "This violation specifically breaks our drug-free workplace policy."
- "Because of your tardiness, I had to pull Jim out of the mailroom to cover your job."

Step 3: Specify the Required Changes

The next step is to explain to your employee exactly what he or she needs to do to correct the behavior. At this time, you will also tell the employee that his or her behavior must be in accordance with an established performance standard or company policy.

Here are some examples of the third part of your discipline script:

- "You must bring your performance up to the standard of 40 reports per month or better immediately."
- "You will be required to set an appointment with the company's employee assistance program for drug counseling."
- "I expect you to be in your seat, ready to work, at 9:00 A.M. every morning."

Step 4: Outline the Consequences

No discipline is complete without a discussion of the consequences if the unacceptable behavior continues. Make sure that your message is clear and that your employee understands it.

THE REAL WORLD

Although it's seldom the most desirable aspect of managing, discipline is a serious responsibility that no effective manager should shirk. Rarely does a bad situation automatically correct itself, and often things will get worse if left unchecked. By correcting employees quickly, objectively, and constructively, you have the opportunity to keep a small problem from becoming a major problem and can even make the experience a positive one from which the employee can learn, appreciate, and grow. To disarm your criticism, it is easy to use a disclaimer such as, "I may be wrong about this, but it seems as though your motivation has dropped of late. Is there something you'd like to discuss?" If the employee dismisses your concern, focus more specifically on your evidence that a problem exists: "I've been getting complaints about you from some of our customers." If nothing else, because the situation is a concern for you, it needs to be a concern for the employee. Like any skill, the more you practice discipline and giving corrective feedback, the better you become at it.

Here are some examples for the fourth part of your script:

- "If you can't meet the standard, you'll be reassigned to the training unit until your skills improve."
- "If you refuse to undergo drug counseling, you'll be suspended from work without pay for three days."
- "If you're late again, I will request that my boss give you a formal reprimand."

Step 5: Provide Emotional Support

During the course of a discipline, your employee would benefit from an emotional boost. Support your employee's efforts to improve in a sincere and heartfelt way.

Here are some examples of how to wrap up your discipline script:

- "But I'm sure you'll be able to avoid that—I know you can do better!"
- "We need you and our customers need you—let's find you the help you need."
- "But I'm sure we can avoid that situation—I'm counting on you to turn this around!"

Put It All Together

After you develop the five parts of your discipline script, put them together into a unified statement. This statement is what you'll deliver to your employees in a discipline meeting. While you should discuss the surrounding issues in some detail, make your script be the heart of the discipline session.

- "You produced only 25 service reports last month instead of the required standard of 40 per month. Because of your below-standard performance, the work unit didn't meet its overall targets for the month. You must bring your performance up to the standard of 40 reports per month or better immediately. If you can't meet the standard, you'll be reassigned to the training unit until your skills improve. But I'm sure you'll be able to avoid that—I know you can do better!"
- "You failed the drug test that you took on Friday. This violation specifically breaks our drug-free workplace policy. You'll be required to set an appointment with the company's employee assistance program for drug counseling. If you refuse to undergo drug counseling, you'll be suspended from work without pay for three days. We need you and our customers need you—let's find you the help you need."
- "You have been late to work every day this week. Because of your tardiness, I had to pull Jim out of the mailroom to cover your job. I expect you to be in your seat, ready to work, at 9:00 A.M. every

morning. If you're late again, I will request that the general manager issue a formal reprimand in your case. But I'm sure we can avoid that situation—I'm counting on you to turn this around!"

CREATING EMPLOYEE IMPROVEMENT PLANS

Performance improvement plans are a crucial part of the discipline process because they set definite steps for employees to undertake to improve performance within a fixed period of time.

If employee performance transgressions are minor then creating a performance plan is generally not necessary. Also, because most instances of misconduct must by nature be corrected immediately or else, performance improvement plans are generally not appropriate for correcting employee misconduct. However, if your employee's poor performance is habitual and you've selected counseling or more severe discipline, a performance plan is clearly appropriate.

A performance improvement plan has three parts:

1. *Goal statement:* The goal statement tells your employees exactly what it will take to make satisfactory improvement. The statement is tied directly to your employee's performance standards, for example, "Completes all his assignments on or before agreed deadlines," or "Is at her station ready to work at exactly 9:00 A.M. every day."
2. *To be effective, plans need definite completion dates with fixed milestones along the way.*
3. *Required resources/training:* If the employee will need additional resources or training to improve performance, they will be summarized here.

Here's a sample performance improvement plan for a worker who makes repeated errors in typed correspondence:

George Tyerbyte's Performance Improvement Plan

Goal Statement

- Complete all drafts of typed correspondence with one or fewer mistakes per document.

Schedule for Attainment

- George must meet the above goal within one month after the date of this plan.

Required Resources/Training

- George will be immediately enrolled in the company refresher course in typing and reviewing correspondence. This training must be successfully completed no later than two weeks after the date of this plan.

Rather than assuming the plan will be acted on by your employee, follow up to ensure that they are making progress toward the goals that you both agreed to.

Help your employees implement their improvement plans by scheduling regular progress reporting meetings with them, on a daily, weekly, or monthly basis. More extensive improvement plans necessitate more frequent follow-up. Progress meetings such as these serve two important functions:

1. They provide you with the information that you need to assess your employees' progress toward meeting their plans.
2. They demonstrate to your employees that their progress is important to you, and thus should be prioritized.

Create performance improvement plans and put them to work with your employees. Reward your employees for achieving their plans, but beware of employees who improve under your watchful eye, but who return to their old ways when they think you're not looking any longer. If an employee can't maintain his or her required performance standards, you may want to consider whether he or she is really suited to work for your organization.

———————————— **POP QUIZ!** ————————————

There is more to disciplining employees than simply punishing them for every conceivable transgression on the job. Reflect for a few moments on what you have learned in this chapter; then ask yourself the following questions:

1. What is your philosophy of employee discipline?
2. Are you fair and objective when you discipline employees? If not, why not?
3. Do you play favorites with certain employees? Who and why?
4. In what ways do you differentiate the treatment of performance problems from misconduct?
5. How are employee improvement plans structured in your organization?

CHAPTER 15

Terminating Employees

IT'S A NEW WORLD OUT THERE . . .

Firing and . . .

How to conduct terminations the right way.

Termination: The final disciplinary step.

Reasons for termination.

Dealing with layoffs and downsizings.

Ensuring fairness of terminations.

How to fire employees.

WHEN ALL ELSE FAILS . . .

Unless you're Donald Trump, one of the most difficult jobs for any manager is to fire an employee. And no matter how many times you do it, firing employees is never something a manager looks forward to doing. But terminating employees is a part of every manager's job, and it's a skill that you can learn and improve.

Sometimes, no matter how much you try to help someone succeed in your organization, there's nothing you can do to save him or her. Terminations aren't limited only to your discretion, sometimes employees "fire" themselves. If you're lucky, they will give you two weeks' notice.

In this chapter, we'll consider that most permanent form of employee discipline—termination—what they are, and how to do them the right way. We'll explore the difference between a layoff and a firing and take a close look at the importance of documentation to support your actions.

DIFFERENT FLAVORS OF TERMINATIONS

There is more than one kind of termination—they vary depending on the situation. To begin, there are two major categories of employee termination: voluntary and involuntary. A voluntary termination is a termination that an employee performs of his or her own free will. An involuntary termination is a termination carried out against the will of the employee. In the sections that follow, we'll consider each of these categories in detail.

Voluntary Terminations

As you read this, you might wonder to yourself, "Why would someone go through a voluntary termination?" Actually, employees have a variety of different reasons to want to terminate their own employment. Employees often quit their jobs when they find better promotional or pay opportunities with another firm, or when they get tired of being stuck in dead-end work situations or enmeshed in personality conflicts with their manager or other employees. Employees also terminate voluntarily because of emotional stress, family needs, moves to other cities or states, and a wide variety of other personal reasons.

The most common reasons that employees voluntarily leave are:

- *Resignation (unencouraged):* When an employee decides to quit his or her position with no prodding or suggestion to do so from his manager or other leaders in the organization, this is considered to be an unencouraged resignation. While an occasional unencouraged resignation is to be expected in any organization, when there is an ongoing trend for employees to voluntarily resign, you should quickly act to find out why. If a particular store is experiencing high turnover, for example, this is a clear warning of problems, which could include anything from a bad supervisor to inadequate staffing to poor work conditions.

- *Resignation (encouraged):* When an employee is asked to leave the organization by his or her supervisor or other leaders in the organization, this is considered to be an encouraged resignation. Encouraged resignations are often used as face-saving measures for employees who are about to be fired. It's a win-win—the employer smoothly eases the employee out of the organization while the employee gets to appear that the termination was all his idea.

- *Retirement:* Retirement—when employees reach the end of their career and decide to terminate their employment once and for all—is something that we all dream of. As people live longer, as Social Security becomes less reliable, and as the cost of living continues to climb, retirements are being deferred to increasingly older ages.

Involuntary Terminations

Voluntary terminations are easy; involuntary terminations—those carried out against the will of the employee—are not so easy. The majority of involuntary terminations fall within two different categories:

- *Layoffs:* When an organization's owners or management team decide to terminate employees for financial or other (usually) cost-cutting reasons, this is considered a layoff, also known as a reduction in force. A common example is the company that loses a number of key contracts—along with the revenue that would have come from them—and that has little choice but to reduce payroll and related personnel costs (often the greatest expense for most organizations) through layoffs. Layoff policies differ among different organizations; in some, the last employee hired is the first to go—in others, employee performance (or lack thereof) determines layoffs. Most organizations give hiring preference to laid-off employees if and when financial health is restored and hiring again begins.
- *Firing:* The famous words "you're fired!" are spoken when a manager decides that an employee's performance shows no hope of improving or when they commit an act of misconduct (stealing, physical violence, etc.) that is so serious that termination is the only choice.

In the United States, companies have traditionally had the right to terminate employees for any reason whatsoever—including no reason—unless a contract between employer and employee expressly prohibits such an action. This termination-at-will rule, or "at-will" for short, has been significantly eroded—particularly in cases of discrimination against employees—as a result of court decisions, union agreements, and recent state and federal laws. At-will remains on the books in some states, and a number of companies require prospective employees to sign a statement confirming termination-at-will when they are hired.

The Civil Rights Act of 1964, the Equal Employment Opportunity Act of 1991, and the Age Discrimination in Employment Act of 1967, and others prohibit terminating employees because of their age, race, gender, color, religion, national origin, and other specific reasons. Ignore these prohibitions at your peril—the mere appearance of discrimination in the termination process can get you into some very serious trouble.

WHY TERMINATE YOUR EMPLOYEES?

There are a number of employee behaviors that are simply unacceptable and that merit firing—sometimes on the spot. This category of behaviors—*intolerable offenses*—merit immediate action, without the benefit of the system of progressive discipline described in Chapter 14, no verbal counseling, no written warning, and no reprimand or suspension. Such offenses include:

- *Verbal abuse of others:* Your employees have a right to work in an environment where they will not be physically or mentally abused. Cursing, repeated verbal harassment, malicious insults, and similar behaviors are not acceptable, and after giving fair warning, you are free to fire employees who engage in this behavior. Not only that, but if you don't take action by firing a repeat abuser, you could be personally sued for allowing this behavior to go on.
- *Incompetence:* Not every employee is competent at his or her job, in fact, some are outright incompetent. If your employees still can't

perform their duties at an acceptable level of competence—even after repeated attempts on your part to help bring their skills up to par—you are certainly justified in firing them.

- *Repeated, unexcused tardiness:* In most organizations, employee schedules are carefully choreographed to ensure that vital systems are staffed and customers served during agreed-upon times. Late employees upset these schedules, interfering with the organization's ability to get work done. If employees continue to be late to work—after being warned that further late arrivals will put their jobs in jeopardy—then termination is the right solution.

- *Insubordination:* When an employee consciously refuses to carry out his or her assigned duties, this is grounds for immediate termination without warning.

- *Physical violence:* Especially in these post-9/11 days, most companies take employee-initiated physical violence and threats of violence very seriously. Not only do employees have the right to a safe workplace; employers have the duty to provide it. There is just no place for violence or threats of violence in any workplace and you should not tolerate it.

- *Theft:* Employees caught stealing—whether company property, or the property of clients or coworkers—can be terminated immediately and without warning.

- *Intoxication on the job:* Being drunk or under the influence of drugs on the job is sufficient grounds for immediate termination. Many companies take a more compassionate route, however, offering their employees the option of undergoing counseling with an employee assistance program or enrolling in a program such as Alcoholics Anonymous instead of being terminated.

- *Falsification of records:* Falsifying records—providing fraudulent information during the hiring process (fake schools, degrees, previous jobs, etc.) and producing other fraudulent information during the course of employment (fake expense reports, falsified timecards, cheating on examinations, etc.)—is also grounds for immediate dismissal.

REASONS THAT SOME MANAGERS AVOID THE INEVITABLE

Terminating an employee is not fun and few managers enjoy it. Regardless, it can be helpful to remember this old saying: Hire slow, fire quick. When you've got a serious employee problem that can't be resolved, then don't hesitate to terminate the employee as soon as it becomes clear that that is the best alternative.

Here are some common reasons why managers avoid terminating employees:

- *Fear of the unknown:* The firing process can be a scary one—not just for the employee being terminated, but also for the manager doing the terminating. Every manager has to experience a first time, and it helps to sit in on a termination or two with an experienced manager (as a witness) before you conduct your first. Be sure to discuss the termination process in detail with your human resources representative to understand how it works in your organization.
- *Emotional involvement:* Sometimes you're going to be forced to terminate a friend or trusted associate. It's bad enough to have to terminate an employee, but terminating someone you like is ten times worse. The fact that they may be performing poorly doesn't make it any easier.
- *Possibility of legal action:* The fear of legal action is often enough to cause any manager to freeze up when it comes time to terminate

> **Ask Bob and Peter:** What do you put down on an employment application when you have been terminated from a job and you have no idea why? I'm in the process of filing a lawsuit on the issue; however, I'm also looking for a new job. In applying for employment, they ask if you have been fired and why. I have no idea why. Now what?
>
> You have no choice but to be truthful in filling out applications for employment. Not only is it the ethical thing to do, but also companies must reserve the right to terminate you if you lie on your application. Assuming you were terminated unjustly, in the box that asks you to explain why you were terminated, consider writing or typing in these words: "Contact me for details." If your potential employer is impressed enough with your resume and qualifications, he or she will give you the opportunity to explain exactly what happened—probably in a preinterview telephone call where you'll have the opportunity to present your side of the story. Caution: Keep your explanation brief and upbeat (e.g., "I got a new manager who had a different opinion on how my areas of responsibility should be handled")—don't drag a prospective employer through a prolonged airing of all of your previous employer's shortcomings. No employer wants to hear that.

an employee. Truth be told, you should worry in today's legal environment. This is why, before you fire an employee, you should be able to justify it.

LAYING OFF EMPLOYEES

Layoffs are fundamentally different from firings because the employees who are terminated are generally not at direct fault. The real culprits are mostly external factors such as changes in markets, mergers and acquisitions, and the pressures of a more competitive global marketplace. These are employees who have done no wrong; these are employees who were simply in the right place at the wrong time.

The following steps will guide you through the layoff process:

Step 1: Determine the extent of the problem and figure out what departments will be affected. How much money are we talking? How long are the poor business conditions that led to this problem projected to last? Are there alternatives that will allow the company to take other cost-saving approaches and avoid a layoff?

Step 2: Freeze hiring. When preparing for a layoff, it's important to quickly put a lid on discretionary spending. As hiring new employees is one of the most expensive sources of discretionary spending, it should be one of the first things stopped. If you do have to hire to staff essential positions (for example, front-line sales staff) which have become vacant, be sure to first consider previously laid-off employees before going outside the organization.

Step 3: Prepare tentative lists of employees to be laid off. Once you understand the extent of the problem and which departments will be affected, you'll need to determine which employees to lay off. Consider which employees have the most skill and experience in the areas that the organization needs and which employees have the least. The first employees to go in a layoff are usually those employees whose skills and experience are not most essential, or those who have been most recently hired.

Step 4: Notify all employees of planned layoffs in advance. As soon as a layoff is certain, immediately inform your employees about it. Present the financial and other problems that your organization faces, and ask your employees for cost-cutting suggestions. In many cases, employee cost-cutting suggestions have saved organizations enough money to postpone or even avert planned layoffs.

Step 5: Prepare a final list of employees to be laid off. The next step is to prepare a rank-ordered list of employees to be laid off. Some companies give preference to permanent employees over temporary ones and include seniority or performance in the formula for determining who will be laid off. If you don't have a standard layoff policy, then consider your employees' experience and how long they've been with the organization in determining who will have to go. Be particularly careful not to discriminate against protected workers—older employees, for example—who are good performers.

Step 6: Notify affected employees. By now, speculation is probably rampant about what employees will be let go and which will be invited to stay. As soon as your list is finalized, notify the affected employees. While actual terminations should always be conducted in private meetings, the initial notification of layoffs can be conducted effectively in group or company-wide meetings.

Step 7: Terminate. Conduct private, one-on-one termination meetings with employees to finalize the layoffs. Collect keys, identification badges, and any company-owned equipment and property and explain severance packages, continuation of benefits, and any other company-sponsored termination programs as appropriate. Finally, escort the laid off employees out of the facility (you can do this personally or have a security guard or human resources representative fill the role) and wish them well.

Step 8: Rally the "survivors." No layoff is truly complete until you have an "all-hands" meeting to rally your remaining employees and to let them know that you are committed to avoiding future layoffs.

THE REAL WORLD

There's a saying, "It never gets better than at the beginning," and sometimes, even the best of intentions will still fail. When this happens with an employee who is not working out, it is best to cut your losses early rather than to give that person an undue number of chances to redeem himself or herself. Be honest and fair, but remember that you don't owe a job to anyone. Just because employees are in positions in your firm does not make those positions theirs. If the person is not working out for you, inevitably the job is not working out for them, either, and although changing jobs can be traumatic for most employees, staying in one that is not working out is far worse.

FIRING HUMANELY

Is it possible to terminate an employee in a respectful and humane way? The quick answer is yes. Here are some ways to do just that:

- *Give employees the benefit of the doubt.* Before you terminate an employee, first give him or her a fair chance to bring his or her performance up to standard. If you're firing an employee because of an intolerable offense such as stealing or insubordination, be absolutely certain that the employee did what he or she is accused of doing. Err on the side of trusting your employees rather than assuming that they are all out to take advantage of your good nature.
- *Make it clear when expectations aren't being met.* Don't allow small problems to snowball into large problems—problems that require termination. Discuss minor problems—and their proposed fixes—with your employees when they are still minor. Be sure to document these discussions in writing—not just for clarity and reinforcement, but to provide evidence that you have given your employees fair warning.

- *Act quickly to dismiss.* When an employee isn't working out, the sooner that you deal with the situation, the better. Instead of hoping your employees will improve, consider whether they really are, in fact, improving. If you decide it makes sense to terminate, you can still be gracious: "I thought things would work out, but they haven't and we're going to have let you go."

MAKING YOUR TERMINATION STICK

It's bad enough that you've got to fire an employee without then getting dragged through the courts on a charge of wrongful termination. A manager's minor oversight or major indiscretion can lead to substantial monetary judgment in favor of the terminated employees.

It's therefore particularly important that, before you fire an employee for cause, you make sure that you can meet the following criteria:

- *Documentation:* When it comes to terminating an employee, document, document, and then document some more. If the employee is being terminated because of performance shortcomings, you had better have the performance data to back up your assertions. If you're firing an employee for falling asleep on the job, then you had better have proof that this particular employee intentionally meant to bed down during his or her shift. Believe us: You can never have too much documentation.
- *Fair warning:* Did you communicate your employees' performance standards clearly and seek their understanding and agreement with them? Did you clearly describe your expectations, along with the penalties for not meeting them? Have you given your employees fair warning to improve their performance or behavior or be subject to termination? Except in the case of intolerable offenses, you should plan to put your employees on notice that their continued employment is in jeopardy unless they turn things around—and soon.

- *Response time:* Have you given your employees enough time to improve before you fired them for performance or behavioral issues? Employees with minor issues should be given more time to improve their performance or behavior than employees with major issues. If the employee is going to be expected to improve performance on a complex and lengthy project, however, understand that demonstrating improvement may take weeks or even months.

- *Reasonableness:* Are your termination policies and practices reasonable, and are the performance standards that you set reasonably achievable? The test here is whether or not you have set the bar so high that no one could achieve it.

- *Avenues for appeal:* In the United States, our basic sense of fairness requires that terminated employees have some avenue available to present their side of the story to higher management. On some occasions, direct managers or supervisors really do "have it out" for employees, or they are too emotionally involved. This can cause errors in judgment that a higher up will quickly see and have the opportunity to correct.

TERMINATING IN THREE STEPS

Employees are ultimately responsible for their performance and behavior, not you. Assuming that you have given your employee fair warning, and the employee has chosen to continue the misconduct or below-standard performance, then you have little choice but to terminate.

When firing employees, keep these two key goals in mind:

1. *Employees deserve a clear explanation for the firing.* Many employees file wrongful termination lawsuits simply to find out the "real" reason they were fired. Tell them—before you're sued, not after.

2. *Employees deserve to have their dignity respected throughout the termination process.* These are people we're talking about, after

all—mothers, fathers, sisters, and brothers. Treat terminated employees the same way you would hope to be treated.

The actual firing should take place in your office or other private location. Figure on setting aside approximately 5 to 10 minutes for the meeting. It's a smart idea to have a witness with you when you terminate an employee—preferably someone of the same sex as the person to be terminated.

There are three steps for firing an employee, including:

Step 1: Tell the employee that he or she is being terminated. Don't beat around the bush; tell your employee that he or she is fired. Firmly tell the employee that the decision is final and not subject to appeal. In most cases, the announcement should come as no surprise because he or she has already been put on notice for performance or behavioral shortcomings. Still, whether or not it's expected, getting fired is still a shock to even the most hardened employee.

Step 2: Explain exactly why the employee is being terminated. If the firing is the result of misconduct, describe the policy that was broken and what the employee did to break it. If the firing is due to a failure to meet performance standards, remind the employee of past counselings and attempts to correct his or her performance and the subsequent incidents that led to the decision to fire. Stick to the facts.

Step 3: Announce the effective date of the termination and provide details on the termination process. A firing is normally effective on the day that you conduct your termination meeting. Keeping a fired employee around is awkward for both you and your employee and should be avoided at all costs. Now is the time to describe termination benefits, if any, and to make arrangements for gathering personal effects from the employee's workspace. Run through the termination paperwork with the employee and explain the handling of final wages due.

Expect the unexpected. While one employee might break out in tears at the news, another might start yelling and screaming and throwing things. You can often defuse these situations by applying the following techniques:

- *Empathize with your employee.* Be understanding of your employee's situation and sincerely show your concern for his or her well-being. If your employee becomes emotional or cries, simply hand the person a box of tissues and proceed with the termination.
- *Be matter of fact and firm.* It's your job to maintain a calm, businesslike demeanor throughout the termination meeting. Don't negotiate with your employee or lead him or her to believe that he or she can do something to change your mind. Insist that the decision is final and not subject to change.
- *Keep the meeting on track.* Don't allow the employee to steer the meeting from the main goal of informing him or her about the termination. If the employee becomes abusive or uncontrollable, inform him or her that you will end the meeting immediately if he or she can't maintain control. Be prepared to call security if necessary.

A *termination script* can be a very helpful thing to have during the termination meeting. Not only will it help to ensure that you don't forget to mention an important piece of information, and it will provide one last piece of documentation for your employee's personnel file (which you should retain for at least seven years after terminating the employee). Rehearse your script several times before you go into the termination meeting.

——————————————— **POP QUIZ!** ———————————————

It's better to terminate employees who have no hope of becoming productive members of your team sooner rather than later. Reflect for a few moments on what you have learned in this chapter; then ask yourself the following questions:

1. What are your termination policies?
2. How do you handle layoffs?
3. What kinds of documentation do you pull together before you terminate an employee?
4. Describe how best to conduct an employee termination.
5. How do you handle employees who become upset or belligerent during a termination?

CHAPTER 16

Ethics and Office Politics

IT'S A NEW WORLD OUT THERE . . .

Ethics and . . .

The impact of office politics on organizations.

Understanding values and ethics on the job.

Creating a code of ethics.

The power of office politics.

Who's hot (and who's not).

Managing your boss.

ETHICS AND OFFICE POLITICS

If you've been in business for any time at all, you know that ethics and office politics are very powerful forces in any organization. *Ethics* is the framework of values that employees use to guide their behavior. Unfortunately, people are not perfect, and ethics is something that's often absent in organizations, as the string of relatively recent business failures attributed to less than sterling ethics in some seemingly upstanding businesses bears testament to. There's more pressure than ever for managers to model ethical behavior and to ensure that their employees follow in their footsteps, and it's the wise manager who quickly gets with this particular program.

The other powerful force in organizations, *office politics*, represents the relationships that you develop with your coworkers—both up and down the chain of command—that allow you to get tasks done, to be informed about the latest goings-on in the business, and to form a personal network of business associates for support throughout your career. On the positive side, office politics helps ensure that employees work in the best interests of the organization. On the negative side, office politics can degenerate into a competition, where employees concentrate their efforts on trying to increase their personal power at the expense of their coworkers and—ultimately—their organizations.

ETHICS: NOT JUST FOR BREAKFAST ANYMORE

Reading the headlines in any newspaper over the past couple of years might lead you to believe that the vast majority of business leaders must all belong to a big club of liars and cheats. The good news is that the vast majority of business leaders actually do know the difference between right and wrong and, now more than ever, businesses and the leaders who run them are trying to do the right thing. Not only do they want to do the right thing to be on the right side of the ethics fence, but also because it's good for the bottom line.

Ethics is in. And that's not a bad thing for any of us.

Defining Ethics

Ethics are standards of beliefs and values that guide conduct, behavior, and activities. Ethics provide boundaries for our actions and help us do the right thing—not just *talking* about doing the right thing, but really doing it.

While we may disagree on exactly what qualities ethical people exhibit on the job, we can generally agree that some or all of the following personal qualities constitute ethical behavior:

- Honesty.
- Integrity.
- Impartiality.
- Fairness.
- Loyalty.
- Dedication.
- Responsibility.
- Accountability.

Remember: When you set an example as an ethical leader, your employees will be encouraged (and expected) to follow your example, too. Managers have a responsibility to try to define an organization's culture and ethics, live up to them, and encourage others to adopt them.

Creating a Code of Ethics

Many organizations have found that it's best not to leave ethics to chance. Rather than let their employees feel their way around in the dark or be left uncertain whether a particular practice is ethical, these organizations have adopted their own written codes of ethics.

A code of ethics is a complement for existing company policies and procedures, not a replacement for them. While most people would probably agree that stealing, sharing trade secrets, sexually harassing a coworker, and other unethical behavior are unacceptable, putting these standards into writing gives this understanding real weight—especially when breaching them may be grounds for dismissal.

A good code of ethics is built on the following foundation:

1. Compliance with internal policies and procedures.
2. Compliance with external laws and regulations.
3. Direction from organizational values.
4. Direction from individual values.

Specifically, a code of ethics must address some very specific issues in addition to the more generic ones listed above. Here are some of the most common issues addressed by typical codes of ethics:

- Equal opportunity.
- Sexual harassment.
- Diversity.
- Privacy and confidentiality.
- Conflicts of interest.
- Gifts and gratuities.
- Employee health and safety.

It's not enough, however, to simply have a code of ethics. The people in your organization must breathe life into it by also *living* it. The best code of ethics in the world is worthless if it's just filed away and never used.

What's in a Comprehensive Code of Ethics?

According to the Ethics Resource Center web site (www.ethics.org), a comprehensive code of ethics has seven parts:

1. *A memorable title:* Examples include Pricewaterhouse's "The Way We Do Business" and the World Bank Group's "Living Our Values."
2. *Leadership letter:* A cover letter briefly outlines the content of the code of ethics and clearly demonstrates commitment from the very top of the organization to ethical principles of behavior.
3. *Table of contents:* The main parts of the code are listed by page number.
4. *Introduction-prologue:* This part explains why the code is important, the scope of the code, and to whom it will apply.
5. *Statement of core values:* The organization lists and describes its primary values in detail.
6. *Code provisions:* This part is the meat of the code, the organization's position on a wide variety of issues including topics such as sexual harassment, privacy, conflicts of interest, gratuities, and so forth.
7. *Information and resources:* Places that employees can go for further information or for specific advice or counsel.

LIVING ETHICS

It's one thing to have a code of ethics; it's another thing altogether to behave ethically in all of your day-to-day business transactions and relationships. Ethical challenges are everywhere in business, and it's your job to apply your organization's code of ethics, your own personal ethics, and no small amount of common sense as you work through them. Here are some common ethical dilemmas; how would you handle them?

- A vendor gives you free tickets to a sold-out NFL football game.
- An employee begs you not to discipline him for breaking company rules.

- You find out that an employee knowingly sold an unnecessary product to a client in order to reach a sales quota and win a trip to the Bahamas.
- You discover that one of your best employees didn't graduate from college as she claimed in her job application.
- You know that a product you sell doesn't do everything your company claims it does.

Every day we our faced with all sorts of ethical choices on the job. Here are six keys to making better ethical choices in your own work life (ETHICS):

1. *Evaluate* circumstances through the appropriate filters (e.g., culture, laws, policies, circumstances, relationships, politics, perception, emotions, values, bias, and religion).
2. *Treat* people and issues fairly within the established boundaries. Fair doesn't always mean equal.
3. *Hesitate* before making critical decisions.
4. *Inform* those affected of the standard/decision that has been set/made.
5. *Create* an environment of consistency for yourself and your working group.
6. *Seek* counsel when there is any doubt (but from those who are honest and whom you respect).

OFFICE POLITICS

How political is your office or place of work? If you're like most managers, you can likely relate more than one or two stories of business associates who have had their careers trashed by being on the wrong end of a political maneuver by someone in their organizations. No matter how much you might try to prevent it, when your organization has two or more employees, you can be sure that office politics are going to be a part of the equation.

ASK BOB AND PETER: How would you deal with a copartner in the company who's been backstabbing me in front of other employees?

The first thing we would do is confront her with her behavior—have you talked to her about this yet? Don't beat around the bush. Give her specific incidents, dates, names, and so on. Tell her in no uncertain terms that you will not tolerate the behavior. Business is built on relationships. Relationships are built on respect and trust. There is no way that you can trust someone who does not respect you. Your copartner clearly does not. Clearing the air gives you both a chance to repair and rebuild your relationship from which you both can benefit.

While the term *office politics* might have a negative connotation to many workers, the fact is that office politics are generally a very positive force in an organization. Office politics—the nature of the relationships that you develop with your coworkers—are the basis for getting things done. However, at their worst, office politics can degenerate in a nasty, competitive, and self-serving mess.

Before you dive into the political waters in your office, make sure that you keep your head above water by assessing your organization's political environment.

Assessing Your Organization's Political Environment

Before jumping into any potentially dangerous or volatile situation, it's always best to first assess what's going on—preferably at a distance first, before you get too close up. Here are some ways to do just that:

- *Find out how others who seem to be effective get things done.* Effective people have already figured out the lay of the land, they know how the organization's political machine works, and how to get things done within it. Model your behavior (or at least take lots of notes) after people who are particularly effective at getting tasks done in your organization's political environment.

- *Observe how others are rewarded for the jobs they do.* Who gets rewarded in your organization, when, and for what reasons? Is credit given to the entire project team that made something good happen, or does only the manager get his or her picture in the company newsletter? How your company rewards behavior tells you exactly what behavior is expected of employees in your organization.

- *Ask questions.* One of the best ways to assess your organization's political environment is simply to ask your coworkers how things work. It's amazing what you can learn if you ask the right questions (and swear yourself to secrecy).

- *Observe how others are disciplined for the jobs they do.* Do managers in your organization criticize employees in public or in front of their coworkers? Are all employees held accountable for decisions, actions, and mistakes, or just the employees who are not well liked by management? Observe and then act. If your management does not encourage risk taking, for example, you might want to avoid engaging in behavior that might be considered risky.

- *Consider how formal the people in the organization are.* Is your organization casual or formal? Are employees encouraged to act and dress casually, and to focus on behavior rather than appearance, or are they encouraged to be buttoned down on the job? Gauging the formality will help you understand how you need to act to conform to the expectations of others.

IDENTIFYING KEY PLAYERS

Key players are the politically astute individuals who make things happen in an organization, and it's a good idea to get to know them and perhaps even to become their trusted ally and friend. But keep in mind that, sometimes, influential people don't hold influential positions.

Susan might be an associate vice president, but have little power over people or budgets beyond her sort of impressive title, while her employee, Cathy (who does not have an impressive title), commands a huge amount of real power because of her position as president of the local union.

Here are some things to look out for as you work to identify the key players in your organization:

- Which employees are sought for advice in your organization?
- Which employees are considered by others to be indispensable?
- Whose office is located closest to those of the organization's top management, and whose are located far away (perhaps around the world)?
- Who regularly eats lunch with the president, the vice presidents, and other members of the upper management team, or joins them for dinner or drinks after work?

Key players in your organization can be organized under a number of different categories, depending on their personalities and how they get things done. Here are some of the most common:

- *Movers and shakers:* These are the people who really get things done in an organization and you can recognize them because their impact usually far exceeds the boundaries of their titles or positions. These are great people to have as mentors or to associate with on and off the job.
- *Corporate citizens:* These are diligent, hardworking, company-loving employees who seek slow but steady, long-term advancement through dedication and hard work. Nothing wrong with that. These folks make great resources for getting information and advice about the organization, and you can almost always count on them for help and support, especially if your ideas are consistent with the best interest of the organization.
- *The town gossips:* You know who these people are: the employees who always seem to know what's going on in the organization.

While gossip may be fun to listen to, assume that anything you actually tell them will be broadcast widely throughout your organization. Be sure to have good things to say about your boss and coworkers when you're in the presence of a gossip.

- *Firefighters:* Every organization has men and women who thrive on being heroes—who like nothing better than to save a project, client, deadline, or whatever that appears to be doomed. It's a good idea to keep these firefighters well informed of your activities so that you don't end up being the subject of their next "fire."

- *The vetoers:* With a simple comment such as, "We tried that and it didn't work," a vetoer can turn all those plans that you labored over for months into a worthless stack of paper. When plagued with vetoers, do your best to keep them out of your decision loop. Find other individuals who can get your ideas approved or find another forum in which to present them—a forum that does not include the vetoer on the invitation list.

- *Whiners:* Whiners—employees are never satisfied with whatever is done for them—personally drive us nuts. Whiners poison the organizations in which they work and their pessimism can be highly infectious. Make a point of being optimistic and avoid whiners like the plague—the best employees gravitate to managers who reward excellence and discourage whining.

COMMUNICATION: REAL OR NOT?

Deciphering the real meaning of communication in an organization is a very important skill for every manager to learn, and it is very much a function of your political environment. To get to the underlying meanings of formal and informal communication, observe behavior, read between the lines, and, when necessary, know how to obtain sensitive information.

ASK BOB AND PETER: What is the best solution to attitude problems and employees who are going around their direct supervisor to me about their problems.

The best solution is to find out why these employees feel that they have to come to you to get their problems solved. Our initial feeling is that the direct supervisor is not doing his or her job in dealing with the issues that he or she is responsible for. Why can't the direct supervisor solve these issues before they get to you? Are your problem employees the real issue, or is it perhaps their supervisor? You should always be available to *any* employee if he or she can't get his or her problems solved by a supervisor. However, if there is an ongoing pattern of employees bypassing a particular supervisor to bring their problems to you, then you should take a close look at what the employee's supervisor is (or is not) doing.

Actions Speak Louder than Words

Communication and the actual behavior that follows are two separate things—sometimes related, and sometimes not. Do others do what they say they are going to do? Do they walk the talk? Pay close attention to the behavior of the communicator to get a feel for their real values and priorities.

Consider the situation when your boss tells you that she loves your work and has recommended you for a bonus. Great, you think—that would be terrific. But, weeks pass, months pass, and no bonus is forthcoming. What really happened? Was she really being sincere with you? Did she submit the necessary paperwork or talk about it with her boss? Did she just get busy and forget? The answers to these questions and others like them will give you with a quick indication of whether your boss is real—and how you rate in the bigger scheme of things.

Reading between the Lines

While not out-and-out lying, people in business often use subtle disinformation to avoid dealing with unpleasant situations such as layoffs, firings, or loss of critical markets or customers. Read between the lines of corporate communications, memos, and press releases to see if there are any other messages that aren't being told. Consider this benign notice in a company newsletter announcing an upcoming reorganization:

> Congratulations to Susan Taylor who unexpectedly retired last week to spend more time with her family. Tom Waco steps into her large shoes as our new Vice President of Engineering and Design.

Reading between the lines, you might realize that the real memo reads something like this:

> Susan Taylor, who had a huge problem getting to work on time over the past several years, finally did something bad enough to justify getting fired. Don't bother dropping by her office to offer your condolences, she was forced to pack up her belongings last Friday and was escorted off the premises by our security guard. Tom Waco, on the other hand, always gets to work on time, and he sometimes stays late, too. This promotion fits in very well with Tom's personal career plan, and it wouldn't hurt your career at all to offer your congratulations in person sometime this week. A nice card would be even better.

Probing for Information

It's in your interest to become a trusted listener to as many people as possible in your organization. This requires a lot of trust, however, and it takes time to develop the high levels of trust necessary to get people to open up and to reveal their real feelings. To gain the trust of others,

---

THE REAL WORLD

Every office has ethical issues and politics, some to greater degrees than others. Being aware of these challenges and operating effectively within them can help you be successful in your job and your career. But avoid being sidetracked by the negative or the personal issues that can undermine your success. Realize that there may be a day when someone seemingly less committed and deserving gets a promotion that you felt you deserved for reasons you don't agree with. Remember that there will be other opportunities if you stay the course and continue to produce results, and resist becoming bitter or disillusioned with the organization or the people in it. If the situation persists and you continue to feel undervalued and underutilized, there are many other organizations that are likely to appreciate what you have to offer, and it may be best to find a culture that better fits who you are.

---

you have to demonstrate that you are someone who can be trusted. Breach that trust—even once—and you may never recover it again.

When it comes to probing for information from your coworkers or others, there are a number of clear guidelines that you should adhere to, including:

- Have at least three ways of obtaining the information.
- Check the information through two sources.
- Promise anonymity whenever possible.
- Generally know the answers to the questions you ask.
- Be casual and nonthreatening in your approach.
- Assume that the initial answer is superficial.
- Ask the same question different ways.
- Be receptive to whatever information you're given.

MANAGE YOUR MANAGER

Successful managers know the importance of managing not just down the chain of command—to their employees—but also up the chain of command, to their bosses and their bosses' bosses. While you're not going to sign off on your boss's next pay increase, you can have a significant influence on his or her decisions. Here are three of the most effective techniques for managing your manager:

- Keep your manager informed of your successes, and of the successes of your employees.
- Support your manager in meetings, in public and in private.
- Praise your manager publicly and be sure that the praise gets back to your manager.

Although your relationship with your manager is very important for the development and progress of your own career, you need to cultivate relationships with your manager's bosses too. Perhaps the most important relationship to develop beyond your own manager is with your manager's manager—an individual who is likely to have a very big influence on your future.

Move Ahead with Your Mentors

Mentors (discussed in detail in Chapter 6) can play a very important role in your career. Not only can mentors offer you important career advice as you move up in the organization, but they can also become your advocate in higher levels of the organization—the levels that you don't have direct access to.

Seek out a mentor who has organizational clout and is not shy about touting your merits to other decision makers. Even better, get the support of a number of powerful people throughout the organization. Be forward and assertive in establishing relationships with key people, but proceed slowly, or your intentions provoke suspicion.

Be Trustworthy

Managers love employees who are both loyal and trustworthy. In business, these can be very difficult qualities to find in coworker and employees. By demonstrating that you are trustworthy, you're much more likely to become a valued associate of a bright peer or manager. And by tying yourself to this rising star, there's a good chance that he or she will bring you along for the ride. But be sure to tie yourself to more than one star. You never know when that star you've tied yourself to will burn out or get fired.

—————————————— **POP QUIZ!** ——————————————

Ethics and office politics play important roles in every organization. Reflect for a few moments on what you have learned in this chapter; then ask yourself the following questions:

1. What are your personal values and ethical standards?
2. What conditions would cause you to compromise your standards at work?
3. Describe your organization's code of ethics.
4. In what ways do office politics affect the behavior of your employees? Yourself?
5. What do you (or can you) personally do to try to insulate your employees from the impact of office politics?

Epilogue

We hope you find this book to be a useful reference for your job of managing. We've done our best to focus on real-world answers and applications to the most common issues and challenges facing managers today. Our hope is that this book will be useful to you for years to come as a reference in your job, for a quick review, or as a viable second opinion as you face various management issues and challenges.

Management is not simply a vehicle for implementing advice, however, but a calling. You have an opportunity—and a responsibility—to achieve results and impact others. The best management advice cannot be taught—it must be learned. As you integrate your own experience with the information presented in this book, the job managing will become both easier and more fulfilling.

We wish you much success!

Index